Suppressed Prayers

Suppressed Prayers

*Gnostic Spirituality
in Early Christianity*

Gerd Lüdemann
and Martina Janssen

TRINITY PRESS INTERNATIONAL
HARRISBURG, PENNSYLVANIA

Translated by John Bowden from the German
*Unterdrückte Gebete. Gnostische Spiritualität im frühen
Christentum,* published 1997 by Radius Verlag, Stuttgart,
with substantial expansions and corrections by the
authors.

Library of Congress Cataloging-in-Publication Data

Lüdemann, Gerd.
[Unterdrückte Gebete. English]
Suppressed Prayers : gnostic spirituality in early Christianity /
Gerd Lüdemann and Martina Janssen.
p.   cm.
Includes bibliographical references and index.
ISBN 1–56338–250–4 (pbk. : alk. paper)
1. Gnosticism.   2. Prayers, Early Christian.   3. Spirituality–
–History of doctrines—Early church, ca. 30-600.   I. Janssen,
Martina.   II. Title.
BT1390.L8213   1998
273'.1—dc21   98-33525

First North American Edition 1998
by Trinity Press International
P.O. Box 1321
Harrisburg, PA 17105

Trinity Press International is part
of the Morehouse Group.
Printed in Great Britain

Contents

Preface

After reading my book *Heretics: The Other Side of Early Christianity* (SCM Press and Westminster Press 1996), numerous readers expressed a wish to get to know further original texts by heretics which were excluded by the 'official' church of the second century. Here is a collection of them.

Most of the original documents have been newly translated (from the Greek, Latin, Syriac, Coptic and Mandaean) and compared with existing translations. The translation is meant to be readily understood and seeks to do justice to the poetic forms of expression. Therefore it is often quite free.[1] Furthermore, to help understanding and readability, lines are not numbered within the translations. Incomprehensible sections which are superfluous to the train of thought or which have been preserved only in fragments have been omitted, and longer texts have been abbreviated so as not to bore readers.

The following indications are given:

(...)	Omissions
( )	Additions intended to make the text more comprehensible
(viz.)	Explanations of individual words
[...]	Reconstructions of missing or illegible words and sentences in the original text
* *	Emendations of the original text
+ +	Insertions from other manuscripts.

The introductions give only what is needed to understand the text: further information, bibliographies and other Gnostic documents will be found in the section of 'Additional Material' and in the notes. Explanations of difficult terms are given in context, between brackets, when they are not explained in individual notes.

Roald Zellweger translated the Syrian and Mandaean sources into German or checked existing translations, and has helped towards giving this book its present form with many pieces of information and suggestions. Martina Janssen spent many long afternoons with me in Göttingen translating Coptic Gnostic texts and developed the plan of the book.

This English edition is a corrected and substantially enlarged version of the German original, and has been discussed throughout by the editors and John Bowden.

For all further questions see the German first complete edition of the Nag Hammadi texts by Gerd Lüdemann and Martina Janssen (see bibliography).

Nashville/Göttingen
20 August 1998   Gerd Lüdemann/Martina Janssen

Introduction

Early Christianity did not develop along a single track. Alongside the catholic church of the second century, from which the New Testament canon ultimately derives,[2] there were Christian groups whose literature has only been preserved in scraps, because of the planned obliteration of it by catholic bishops. These groups include the Gnostics, who were branded heretics, suppressed and exterminated along with their followers.

Gnosticism is understood to be a religious current which reached a climax in late antiquity. The Greek word *gnosis* means 'knowledge'. For the Gnostic, knowledge is primarily self-knowledge: the human soul is of heavenly origin. The world which – like all matter – is faulty came into being as the result of a false step by a divine power. The divine soul is imprisoned in the material body and has forgotten its true homeland. By the call of the Saviour, whom the Christian Gnostics identify with Jesus, the soul awakens from its sleep and its drunkenness. It is instructed about its origin and its fall. This knowledge brings it salvation and reunites it with the Pleroma (= fullness[3]) from which it comes.

A 'Gnostic programmatic formula' runs like this: 'Who were we? What have we become? Where were we? Into what have we been thrown? Whither are we hastening? From what are we saved? What is birth? What is rebirth?' (*Excerpta ex Theodoto* 78,2).[4] The Gnostics attempted to find an answer to these questions. However, they did not do so by abstract intellectual exercises or with the help of theoretical systems. Rather, in unsurpassed religious creativity they depicted the history of the human self which in the Gnostic texts is often identified with the human soul or with a spark of light. Thus narrative myths with powerful imagery became the means by which Gnosticism was expressed.

Elements from Judaism, from Greek religion and philosophy, from Near Eastern thought and Iranian religion have found their way into these myths. Anything that could provide a plausible explanation of the origin and situation of human beings in the world and their return to their origin found a place in the Gnostic myths.

Gnosticism is not a uniform current. While the question of the true identity of human beings is common to all Gnostic tendencies, the particular elaboration of the Gnostic myth which is the answer to the Gnostic question differs. It is worth making a fundamental distinction between a monistic and a dualistic Gnosticism. In the former, matter or evil also derives from the deity itself and came into being through divine disobedience or a false step; in the latter, evil is a dualistic power opposing the 'good God'. Most Christian Gnostic systems correspond to the first type of Gnosticism. But they too are not intrinsically uniform and can be divided into different Gnostic 'schools', like Valentinianism, or Sethian or Basilidian Gnosticism.

Gnosticism is not limited to Christianity. There is also a Jewish, an Iranian, an Egyptian and a philosophical Gnosticism. This collection of texts contains predominantly evidence from Christian Gnosticism. At the same time it should be emphasized that Mandaean, Manichaean, Hermetic and Neoplatonic Gnostic writings have also been included.

(*a*) The Mandaeans are the only Gnostic group which still exists today. They live in southern Iraq, predominantly by rivers, which is in keeping with their character as a baptismal sect. The Mandaean religion is shaped throughout by cultic actions (baptism and the mass of the soul). The most important Mandaean writings for this volume are, first, the Ginza (Treasure), which consists of two parts: the first part (Right Ginza = RG) contains eighteen doctrinal treatises; the second part (Left Ginza = LG) deals with the ascent of the soul after death to the realm of light. Liturgical texts which are recited at baptism and in the mass of the soul are the content of the Mandaean Liturgies (= ML). The religious tradition of the Mandaeans is composed in a distinctive East Aramaic dialect.[5]

(b) Manichaeism derives from its founder Mani (216–276/7).[6] It represents a religion which combines Hellenistic, Christian and Iranian elements. Its origin lies in Mesopotamia/Persia. Manichaeism spread as far as India and China – not least as a result of the intensive missionary efforts by Mani.[7] So the literary evidence from the Manichaeans is composed in a variety of languages (Iranian, Turkish, Coptic, Chinese, etc.). The mythology of the Manichaeans is characterized by a strict dualism between light and darkness which is influenced by Iranian religion. Human beings find themselves in the midst of this battle between light and darkness; their self belongs to the realm of light but is imprisoned in the matter of darkness. The liberation of the human soul by the primal human being is the central theme of Manichaean religion.[8] The Manichaeans have left behind a large number of writings.[9] The Manichaean Psalm Book (= MPB) was particularly fruitful for this volume.

(c) The Hermetica are to be seen as a kind of 'religious philosophy' of late antiquity.[10] The Hermetic writings are very interested in Platonic philosophy, but they also show signs of considerable influences from Egyptian and Jewish religion. The central role played by knowledge in the Hermetic writings brings the Hermetica close to Gnosticism; they have often been described as pagan Gnosticism. Some motifs of the Hermetica of the second and third century CE are still interesting today to occult communities. The Hermetic evidence in this volume all comes from the Nag Hammadi discovery (Codex VI) or the Corpus Hermeticum (= CH).

(d) The evidence for Neoplatonic Sethian Gnosticism is to be found above all in the Nag Hammadi writings: the Three Steles of Seth (NHC VII 5), Zostrianos (VIII 1), Marsanes (NHC X 1) and Allogenes (NHC XI 3). These writings have much in common in their description and naming of mythological entities and in their literary form, but above all they are dependent on Neoplatonic thought.[11] As a rule they do not belong to the Christian evidence for Gnosticism;[12] rather, they document a mythological Platonism of a kind that was rejected by the leading Neoplatonists as a Neoplatonic heresy. In all probability they are identical with the 'revelation writings' mentioned by Porphyry in his *Life of Plotinus*, against which Plotinus and Porphyry wrote.[13] The main focus of the criticism from Neoplatonism was the strongly magical character which all these writings have in common (passwords, magical vowels and invocations, sacraments; similarities to the Chaldaean oracles). Central to this Platonizing Gnosticism, which claims Seth as its primal ancestor and founder, is the notion of the ascent which leads to divinization; this largely also determines the literary form of the texts.[14]

Although the Mandaeans, the Hermetists, the Manichaeans and the Neoplatonic Gnostics were not Christian Gnostics, some of their writings are particularly well suited to illustrating the basic notions of Gnosticism.

The religious creativity of the Gnostics clashed with the rigid dogmatism of the representatives of the catholic church. The 'orthodox Christians' saw their pure doctrine of salvation by Christ endangered by the Gnostic views, above all by the fact that for the Gnostics the creator god was a faulty 'copy' of the true, unknown Father. The Gnostic disputing of Christ's suffering also led to bitter reactions on the 'church' side.[15] Thus the reports of the church fathers Irenaeus of Lyons (end of the second century) or Epiphanius of Salamis (c.315–403) are full of polemic against the Gnostics.

But what was the Gnostics' attitude to the Christianity of the catholic church? We know of no suppression of church Christians by Gnostic Christians. For the Gnostics, the doctrine and practice of the church Christians was quite compatible with their own convictions; however, for them the religion of the church Christians represented a 'lower stage' by comparison with Gnostic knowledge. Whereas the church Christian remained at this lower stage of knowledge, the Gnostic sought higher knowledge. That can be illustrated from the Gnostic understanding of baptism:[16] for the Gnostics baptism was an important sacrament, but true salvation was achieved completely only by the sacrament of apolytrosis (salvation). This ritual of salvation is either a sacrament of the bridal chamber, a sacrament of dying, or a holy baptism which surpasses the baptism with water practised by the catholic church.[17]

A sensational discovery made shortly after World War 2 offers us an undistorted look at Gnostic mythology and spirituality. At the end of 1945 near Nag Hammadi, a small town in Upper Egypt, thirteen codices in Coptic were found which for the most part contained Gnostic texts of very different tendencies. This amounted to a rediscovery of Gnosticism. Whereas before the Nag Hammadi discovery Gnosticism was mostly known only through the one-sided and distorting accounts of the church fathers, in these texts the Gnostics finally spoke for themselves. So it is understandable that most of the texts contained in the present collection come from the Nag Hammadi Codices (= NHC). Although the codices are of a late date (fourth century), we must assume that many Nag Hammadi texts contain traditions which go back to the second century CE.[18]

Other collections of texts which were already known in the previous century and contain genuinely Gnostic writings are the Bruce Codex (Books of Jeu; the Untitled Text), the Askew Codex (Pistis Sophia) and the Berlin Codex (Sophia Jesu Christi; Apocryphon of John). The Odes of Solomon (= OdSol) must also be regarded as Gnostic testimonies. These forty-two hymnic texts derive from the piety of a Syrian Gnostic community.[19] Furthermore, Gnostic prayers and hymns can be found in apocryphal acts of apostles, as for example the bridal hymn from the Acts of Thomas. Such stories about the apostles were current among the Gnostics.[20] But in the course of their 'refutation' the church fathers also handed down some original Gnostic documents (e.g. the Naassene Psalm), and these are included here.[21]

Often, in contrast to the literature of the church Christians, we hear female speakers in the Gnostic documents. In this connection mention should be made of the powerful lamentations of the Pistis Sophia or the revelation discourses of feminine Gnostic saviour figures like Bronte and the 'Trimorphic Protennoia'.[22]

The selection of texts offered here does not claim to be a complete documentation of Gnosticism.[23] Its aim is to provide an insight into Gnostic religion. The Gnostic hymns and prayers are particularly suitable for this.[24] They express the Gnostic sense of life in a poetic way.[25] Thus the order in which the texts are presented is not prompted by external considerations but by internal ones, based on the Gnostic programmatic formula in *Excerpta ex Theodoto* 78.2 (see above). The first part of the book contains prayers which give an answer to the Gnostic question of origins (Who were we? Where were we?): at the beginning the Gnostic self was with the good, unknown Father. The second part is orientated on life in the world (What have we become? Into what are we thrown?). The prayers in this section are mostly laments about the suffering of the soul in the world. In the third part, which is the longest, the topic is Gnostic salvation (Whither are we hastening? From what are we saved? What is birth? What is rebirth?). This contains the hymns to the Saviour and the Gnostic prayers which belong in a sacramental context. A fourth part recalls the sorry reality of the hostility to the Gnostics and illustrates the defaming of Gnostic religious practice by the Christians of the church. This makes it clear that, seen in a historical context, the prayers of the Gnostics were suppressed prayers. The Additional Material contains further Gnostic texts on the various parts; like the notes, these add depth to the approach and are meant to prompt further study of Gnosticism.

Suppressed for reasons of dogma and church politics, the Gnostic prayers nevertheless are evidence of an earnest and deep religious sense without which the history of Christianity would certainly have lost some of its richness. Even if the Gnostics were fought against or defamed with every possible means and their prayers fell victim to church censorship, the fascination of Gnosticism remains to the present day.

The Unknown Father

The God of the Gnostics is not the God of this world. The creator of the world to whom the Christians of the church pray is a 'lower God' who out of envy leaves the human soul in ignorance about its heavenly home.[26] The God who brings the Gnostic redemption is the good, unknown Father. He cannot be understood by human efforts. Accordingly it can only be said of him what he is not. This 'negative theology' occupies a good deal of space in all forms of Gnostic literature: at the beginning of a depiction of the Gnostic myth, in many writings there is first a 'definition of the essence' of the unknown, good Father from whom everything has come into being (cf. e.g. Zostrianos [NHC VIII 1] 64,11ff., Allogenes [NHC XI 3] 47,9; 62,1ff.; see also in the Additional Material the Tripartite Tractate, which represents a kind of Gnostic dogmatic; here too there is an enumeration of the properties of God, which is partly composed in the form of a hymn).

'He is' predications

At the beginning of the narrative of the origin of the world in the Letter of Eugnostos and the Apocryphon of John the unknown, good Father is described in hymn-like lists of epithets. Such predications in the 'he is' style are widespread in antiquity and often appear in a text side by side with forms of address in the second person, 'You are'.

From the Letter of Eugnostos

The letter of Eugnostos (NHC III 3 + V 1) is a didactic letter, the content of which is a typically Gnostic cosmogony (doctrine of the origin of the world); at the beginning there is a hymn about the Unknown Father. There is no evident Christian influence.

(NHC III 3; 71,14ff.)
The one who exists is indescribable.
No force knew him, nor power, nor subjection, nor any creature
from the foundation of the world, only he alone (knew himself).

That one is immortal; he is eternal; he has no birth.
For everyone who has a birth will die.
(He) is unbegotten; he has no beginning
For whoever has a beginning has an end.
No one rules over him; he has no name.
For whoever has a name is the creature of another.
(He) is nameless.
(He) has no human form.
For whoever has a human form is the creature of another.

He has his own semblance,
– not like the semblance that we have received and that we have
seen,
but a strange semblance that surpasses all things
and is better than the allnesses.
It looks to every side and sees itself only through itself.

(He) is infinite.
(He) is incomprehensible.
(He) is one who is ever imperishable.
(He) is one who does not have his like.
(He) is unchangeably good.
(He) is without defect.
(He) is one who is everlasting.
(He) is blessed.
(He) is unknowable, whereas he is accustomed to know himself.
(He) is immeasurable.
(He) is undiscoverable.
(He) is perfect, because he has no defect.
(He) is imperishably blessed.
He is called 'Father of the All'.

From the Apocryphon of John

The Apocryphon of John (NHC II 1 + III 1 + IV 1) is a Sethian writing.[27] Apart from the narrative framework, which depicts an appearance of Christ, this writing is divided into two parts. The first part is a revelation discourse of Jesus about the Unknown Father and the origin of the world; like the Letter of Eugnostos the revelation discourse begins with a hymn to the Unknown Father in the 'He is' style;[28] the second part consists of a revelation dialogue between Jesus and John about questions relating to the origin and salvation of human beings. Here the exegesis of Genesis 1–7 plays a major role.

(NHC II 1; 2,26ff.) [He is the one who exists] as [God] and Father of the All,
[the invisible] one who is above [the All],
[who exists as] incorruption (and) [as pure light]
into which no [eye can] look.
He [is the] invisible [Spirit] of whom it is not right [to imagine] him as god[29] or the like.
For he is more than a god, since there is no one above him, for no one is lord over him.
[For he exists] not in some subordination, [for everything] exists in him.
[He is eternal], since he needs [nothing].
For [he] is total perfection.
[He needs nothing] to make him perfect;
[rather] he is always completely perfect in the [light].
He is [illimitable], since no one is [prior to him] to set limits to him.
He is unfathomable, [since there] is no one prior to him [to fathom him.
He is] immeasurable, since there [was] no one [prior to him to measure] him.
[He is invisible, since no one] has seen [him.
He is eternal], since he [exists] eternally.
He is [unutterable, since] no one was able to comprehend him, and (then) to speak [about him].
He is unnameable, since [there is no one prior to him] to name [him].

He is [immeasurable light], which is pure, holy [and immaculate].

He is unutterable, [since he is perfect in] incorruptibility.

(He is) [neither in perfection] nor in blessedness nor in divinity, but he is far superior.

He is neither corporeal [nor is he incorporeal].

He is neither large [nor is he small].

[There is no] way to say,

'How large is he?' or, 'What [is his kind?'], for no one [is able to know him].

He does not belong [among things that exist, but he is] far [superior].

(...)

He is eternity [which gives eternity].

He is life which gives [life].

He is a blessed one who gives blessedness.

He is knowledge which gives knowledge.

[He is] goodness which gives goodness.

[He is] mercy which [gives mercy] and redemption.

He is grace which gives grace.

[Not] because he possesses it,

but because he gives [the] immeasurable, incomprehensible [light].

From the Untitled Text in the Bruce Codex

The Untitled Text is the third Gnostic work in the Bruce Codex, along with the two Books of Jeu. There are also close parallels between these writings in terms of content. They are usually attributed to Barbelo – or Sethian Gnosticism (cf. e.g. the central role which Seth or Setheus plays in this group of writings). But the Nag Hammadi writing Zostrianos (NHC VIII 1) also shows considerable affinity to the Untitled Text in content, though in contrast to Zostrianos, this latter understands itself as a Christian writing.

The Untitled Text is a Gnostic revelation writing which is essentially devoted to the description of the heavenly regions. This writing also contains numerous liturgical sections. These hymns or prayers are usually presented by mythological figures, as is common in Gnostic, above all Sethian, texts (cf. e.g. the Gospel of the Egyptians [NHC III 2], the Apocryphon of John [NHC II 1]). It is conceivable that these prayers and praises also reflect a living Gnostic piety.

First, in chapter 17 there is a hymn to the sole One, which is sung by the Mother of the All and the Forefather and other mythological figures;[30] secondly, in chapter 22 there are forty praises to the Unknown Father. 'You are' predications appear in chapters 7 and 20. To the predication in chapter 20 is added a petition for the sending of incorporeal spirits who are to instruct those born in matter.

Hymn to the unknown God

(Chapter 17)(...)
You alone are the infinite one,
you alone are the deep,
and you alone are the unknowable one;
and you are the one for whom all seek;
and they did not find you;
for no one can know you without your will,
and no one can praise you without your will.
And your will alone is that which became topos (place) for you,
for no one can become topos for you because for all you are their topos.
I pray you to give ordinances to those who belong to the world, and to give regulations to my offspring in accordance with your wish.
And do not allow my offspring to fall into affliction, for no one is ever afflicted by you and no one has known your counsel.
You are the one whom all lack – those within and those outside.
For you alone are an incomprehensible one,
you alone are the invisible one,
and you alone are the insubstantial one,
and you alone are the one who has given characteristics to all creation.
You have manifested them in yourself.

You are the former (demiurge) of those that have not yet
become manifest,
of those whom you alone know
– and we do not know them.
You alone are the one who shows them to us,
so that we should ask of you concerning them,
that you should manifest them,
and we should know them through you alone.
You alone brought yourself to the measure of the hidden
worlds, until they knew you.
It is you who have granted them to know you,
(to know) that you were the one who bore them in your
incorporeal body.
And you have created them, for you have brought forth the
human being in your self-originated mind and in consideration
and in the perfect thought.
This is the human being begotten of the mind, to whom consideration gave form.
It is you who have given all things to the human being.
And he has worn them like clothes, and put them on like
garments, and he has wrapped himself in the creature like a
mantle.
This is the human whom the allnesses pray to know.
You alone have ordained that the human should be revealed
that they know you through him.
For you are the one who has begotten him.
And you have revealed yourself according to your will.
You are the one to whom I pray,
Father of all fatherhoods,
and God of all gods
and Lord of all lords,
the one whom I beseech to give ordinances to those who belong
to me and to my offspring, these, for whom I prepare joy in
your name and in your power.
You alone (are) the ruler and the unchangeable one.
Give me power and I will cause my offspring to know you, (to
know) that you are their Saviour.

Praises

(Chapter 22) I praise you, Father of all fathers of light.
I praise you light-infinite,
(you) who surpass all that is infinite.
I praise you, light-incomprehensible,
(you) who are above all that is incomprehensible.
I praise you, light-unutterable,
(you) who are before all that is unutterable.
I praise you, light-imperishable,
(you) [who] surpass all that is imperishable.
(...)
I praise [you], light-[unutterable].
[I praise] you, light-inconceivable.
(...)
I praise you, [light]-unbegotten.
I praise you, light-self-[existent].

I praise [you], light-forefather,
(you) who surpass all forefathers.
[I praise] you, light-invisible,
(you) who are before [all] that is invisible.
[I] praise you, light-thought,
(you) who surpass all thoughts.
I praise you, light-God,
(you) who are before all gods.
I praise you, knowledge,
(you) who enlighten all knowledge.
I praise you, light-unknowable,
(you) who are before all that is unknowable.
I praise you, light-still one,
(you) who are before all stillness.
I praise [you], light-almighy,
(you) who surpass all that is almighty.
I praise you, light-triple-powered,
(you) who surpass all that has triple power.
I praise you, light-indivisible,
but you are the one who divides all light.

I praise you, light-pure,
(you) who surpass all that is pure.
(...)
I praise you, (you) who understand all things – [no one] understands you.
I praise [you, (you) who] embrace the All – [no one] embraces you.
[I praise] you, (you) who unbegotten have begotten all, – [for] no one has begotten you.

I [praise] you, source of the All [and] of all things.
I praise [you], truly light-self-begotten, you who are before [all] self-begotten ones.
[I] praise you, light-truly unmoved, you [light] for those who have been moved in your [light].

I praise you, silence of all light-silences.
I praise you, saviour of [all] light-saviours,
I praise [you], only light-incomprehensible.

I praise you, (you) who alone are place of all places of the All.
I praise [you], (you) who alone are wise and who alone are wisdom.
I praise [you], alone all-mystery.
[I] praise you, alone [light]-all-perfect.
I praise you, alone untouchable.
(...)
[I praise] you, good one, [you who reveal all] goodness.
I praise you, light, you who alone reveal [all lights].
I praise [you], (you) who awaken [all] understanding, (you) who give life to all souls.
[I praise you], rest of those [...]
(...)
[I] praise you, (you) who dwell [in] every fatherhood from the [beginning] until now. They seek for [you], for you are (the object of) their [quest]. Hear the prayer of [the human being] in every place who [beseeches with] his whole heart.

'You are' predications I

(Chapter 7) He is holy, he is holy, he is holy[31]
this aaa ēēē eee ooo uuu ōōō – that means:
You are alive among the living ones,
and you are holy among the holy ones,
and you are existing among the existing ones,
and you are father among the fathers,
and you are god among the gods,
and you are lord among the lords,
and you are place among the places.
(...)
You are the house,
and you are the one who dwells in the house.
(...)
You exist,
you exist,
Only-begotten,
light and life and grace.

'You are' predications II

(Chapter 20) Give us power so that we make for ourselves aeons
and worlds according to your word which you, Lord, have
agreed with your servant. For:
you alone are the unchanging one,
and you alone are the infinite one,
and you alone are the incomprehensible one,
and you alone are the unbegotten one,
and (you alone are) the self-begotten one,
and (you alone are) the self-father,
and you alone are the unshakable one,
and (you alone are) the unknowable one,
and you alone are the silence,
and (you alone are) the love,
and (you alone are) the source of the All,
and you alone are the non-hylic one,
and (you alone are) the undefiled one,

and (you alone are) the unutterable one with regard to your generation,
and (you alone are) the unthinkable one with regard to your revelation.
Truly, hear me, (you) imperishable Father and immortal Father and God of the hidden things
and you only light and life
and you alone invisible and alone unutterable
and you alone undefiled and you alone invincible
and you alone first existing and he before whom no one exists.

Hear our prayer with which we have prayed to the one who is hidden in all places.
Hear us and send to us incorporeal spirits that they may dwell with us and teach us those things which you have promised to us, and that they may dwell in us and that we may become bodies to them, for it is your will that this should happen. May it happen!
And give a determination to our work and set it up according to your will and according to the determination of hidden aeons. And determine us also – we are yours.

From the Books of Jeu

In the first Book of Jeu (see pp.52f.) there is a ceremony in which Jesus sings the praise of the Father and invites the disciples to reply 'Amen'. There is a similar ritual in the Christ hymn in the Acts of John (see pp.67ff.).

(Chapter 41) (...) Now he said to the twelve (disciples), 'Gather round me all of you.' And they all gathered round him. He said to them, 'Answer me and give praise with me and I will praise my Father for the distribution of all treasures.'
    Now he began to sing praises. He praised his Father and spoke as follows: 'I praise you, you who are of the great name of my Father, whose signs are of the type *(magical signs follow)*,

for you have (with)drawn completely to yourself in truth, until you gave place for this little idea which you have not drawn to yourself, for what now is your will, unapproachable God?'

Then he made his disciples respond 'Amen, Amen, Amen,' three times.

He said to them once again, 'Repeat after me "Amen" after every praise.'

Again he said: 'I sing praise to you, God, my Father, for you are the one who gave place for this little idea to shine out in yourself. What now, unapproachable God?'

Then they said ('Amen') three times.

Then he said: 'I sing praise to you, unapproachable God, for you shone in yourself, whereby you shone according to your will. What now, unapproachable God?'

They said again ('Amen') three times.

'I sing praise to you, unapproachable God, for by your own wish I have shone in you, myself being a single emanation. And I have been poured forth from you. What now is your will, that all these come into being, unapproachable God?'

Thereupon they answered ('Amen') three times, 'unapproachable God.'

There follow further similar praises by Jesus, to each of which the disciples respond with 'Amen, amen, amen.'

Hermetic Prayers

The Hermetists composed impressive prayers: they too are permeated with the notion that one cannot say anything about God and that appropriate praise is possible only in silence.[32]

From the Discourse on the Eighth and the Ninth

The following two prayers come from the 'Discourse on the Eighth and the Ninth' (NHC VI 6).[33] In form this writing is a dialogue beween a revealer and a receiver of revelation.[34] Particularly striking features are the way in which it is stamped by the liturgy (prayer: 55,23–57,25) and ritual (the brotherly kiss: 57,26f.). Also notable is the frequent use of notions which are customary elsewhere in mystery cults (purification, the obligation to keep silent about mysteries received, vision, silence as the climax of the vision, etc.).

(NHC VI 6; 55,23ff.) Let us pray, O my Father:
I call upon you, (you) who rule over the kingdom of power,
whose word comes (to us) as (a) bringing forth of light.
And his words are immortal;
they are eternal and unchangeable.

He is the one whose will generates life for the images in every place.
His nature gives form to substance.
From him the souls of the [eighth and] the angels move (...).
His providence extends to everyone, [...] begets everyone.
He is the one who [...] the aeon among spirits.
He created everything.
He who has himself in himself cares for all things.
He is perfect, the invisible God, to whom one speaks in silence;
his image is moved by being governed, and it governs.
He who is strong in power,
who is exalted above greatness,
who is more elect than (all) glories,
Zōxathazō, aōō ee ōōō ēēē ōōō ōee ōōōōō ooooo ōōōōō uuuuuu ōōōōōōōōōōō Zōzazōth!

Lord, grant us a wisdom from your power that reaches to us, that we may describe to ourselves (mutually) the vision of the Eighth and the Ninth.
We have already reached the Seventh, since we are godfearers and walk in your law; and your will we fulfil at all times.

For we have walked in [your way, and we have] left behind us [...], so that your [vision] may take place. Lord, grant us the truth in the image!
Grant us through the spirit to see the form of the image that has

no defect, and receive from us the type of the Pleroma through
our praise;
and know the spirit that is in us.
For through you the All has been ensouled.
For from you, the unbegotten one, that which is begotten came
into being.
The birth of the self-begotten one takes place through you, the
birth of all begotten things that exist.

Receive from us the spiritual sacrifices which we send up to you
with all our heart and our soul and all our strength.
Save that which is in us and give us the immortal wisdom.

(NHC VI 6; 60,17ff.) I will offer up praise through my heart,
I pray to the end of the All and the beginning of the beginning,
the (object) of the human quest,
the immortal discovery,
the begetter of light and truth,
the sower of the word,[35]
the love of incorruptible life.
A hidden word will not be able to speak of you, Lord.
Therefore my mind wants to sing a hymn to you daily.
I am the instrument of your spirit.
The mind is your plectrum.[36]
Your counsel plays on me.
I see myself.
I have received power from you.
For your love has encountered us.

From Corpus Hermeticum XIII

The Hermetic tractate from which the following hymn is taken deals
with the spiritual rebirth of human beings.[37] The mystic Tat is led by
his mystagogue Hermes in a dialogue about spiritual vision and
divinization. This takes place in rebirth: the human being must leave
behind his body and the changeable, material world and penetrate to

the firm truth, the knowledge of God. This transitory participation in the divine during ecstasy anticipates the union with the divine after death, since the divine powers have entered the one who is reborn.

The process of rebirth is understood in purely spiritual terms as an act of the knowledge of God; there are no references to cult and magic, as there are, for example, in the Discourse on the Eighth and the Ninth (NHC VI 6).

The first hymn is spoken by Hermes (CH XIII 17–20); his disciple Tat responds after a dialogue with a further short hymn (CH XIII 21). Hermes' hymn is introduced with the words 'Hidden Song of Praise (Hymnodia): Fourth Logos'. The numbering is unclear, since there are no previous hymns in the tractate. At best one can recognize a hymnic structure in CH XIII 8–9; however, there is no explicit characterization as in CH XIII 17ff. nor any numbering. We should probably assume that a collection of Hermetic writings existed in which the extant hymns were numbered.

The hymns of Hermes and Tat represent the conclusion and climax of CH XIII; all that follows is a short conclusion, which above all contains a command to maintain secrecy.

(CH XIII 17–20) *Hymn of Hermes:*
Let the whole nature of the cosmos take up (into itself) the sound of the hymn:
Open up, (you) earth,
let every floodgate of the rain open for me,
(you) trees, do not stir!
I am going to offer hymns to the Lord of creation, both to the All and to the One.
Open up, (you) heavens,
and (you) winds, subside.
Let the immortal circle of God accept my word (= prayer) (into itself).
I am going to offer hymns to the one who created all things,
to the one who established the earth and hung up the heaven
and ordained that from the ocean there shall be sweet (= fresh) water for inhabited and uninhabited land
for the nourishment and creation of all human beings,
to the one who has ordained that fire shall shine (forth) for every activity, both for gods and for human beings.

We will all together offer him praise,
to the one who is in the height above all heavens,
the creator of all nature.
This is the eye of the mind.
May he accept the praise of my powers.

(You) powers that are in me, offer hymns both to the One and
to the All,
sing together with my will, all (you) powers who are in me!
Holy knowledge, enlightened through you,
offering hymns through you to the mindful light,
I delight in the joy of the mind.
All (you) powers, offer hymns with me!
And you also, self-control, offer hymns with me!
My righteousness, offer hymns to the righteous one through me!
My community spirit, offer hymns to the All through me!
Offer hymns, truth, to truth,
to the good, good, offer hymns!
Life and light, from you and to you goes praise.
I thank you, Father, energy of the powers!
I thank you, God, power of my energy!
Your word (Logos) offers you hymns through me.
Through me accept the All through the word (Logos), the
spiritual sacrifice!

The powers which are in me cry this out:
to the All they offer hymns,
they fulfil your will.
Your will goes in from you to you, the All!
Accept the spiritual sacrifice from all (viz. reborn).

The All that is in us –
Save, life!
Enlighten, light!
Provide with spirit, God!
For it is your word (Logos) which the mind protects!
Spirit-bearer, demiurge.

You are God!
Your human being calls this
through fire,
through air,
through earth,
through water,
through spirit,
through your creatures!

From your aeon I have found praise and what I seek.
Through your will I have attained rest.
I have seen through your will.

(CH XIII 21) *Hymn of Tat:*
To you, first origin of the begettings,
to God, I send, Tat, spiritual sacrifices.
God, you (are) father,
you (are) lord,
you (are) mind,
accept the sacrifice which you want of me,
according to your willing all is perfected.

From Corpus Hermeticum V

The whole of the fifth tractate in the Corpus Hermeticum deals with
the problem of knowledge of God. God is invisible and cannot be
grasped with the sense organs; knowledge of God can be grasped only
approximately in the understanding. In addition to this motif, which
can be found in many Hermetic writings, there is a further one: the
positive emphasis on God's work in creation. God – who himself cannot be perceived – has made everything else visible and is in all things,
even if he also transcends all things. There is a comparable thought in
the Psalm of Valentinus. There God is praised through his creation (see
below, pp.36f.).

(CH V 10f.) How shall one now praise you,
(how speak) about you or to you?
And where shall I look when I praise you -
above, below, within, without?

There is no (appropriate) way,
no (particular) place is around you,
nor anything else of the things that are.
But all is in you,
all is from you.
You give all and you receive nothing.
You have all and there is nothing that you do not have.

But when shall I sing hymns to you?
It is impossible to grasp your hour or time.

But for what should I sing hymns (to you)?
For the things which you have created,
or for the things which you have not created?
For the things which you have made visible,
or for the things which you have hidden?

But why should I sing hymns to you?
Because I am my own master?
Because I possess something of my own?
Because I am another (than you)?
(No), for you are what I always am.
You are what I always do.
You are what I always say.
You are all and there is nothing else.
What is not, you are.
You are all that has become.
You are (all) that has not become.
(You are) now understanding and (you) have understanding.
(You are) now father, creator.
(You are) now God and are active, you are good and create all
things.

From Poimandres

There is a further Hermetic prayer in Poimandres (CH I), a revelation writing which among other things is about the rapture of the receiver of revelation. In a vision and a revelation dialogue with Poimandres, it is disclosed to him how human beings have come to be in their tragic situation of mortality. At the end of the work the one who has now been initiated into knowledge utters the following prayer:

(CH I 31) Holy is God, the father of the All;
Holy is God, whose will is fulfilled by his own powers.
Holy is God who wills to be known.
And he is known by his own people.

Holy are you, you who with a word have brought forth everything that exists.
Holy are you, whose image all nature has become.
Holy are you, whom nature has not formed.
Holy are you, you who are stronger than any power.
Holy are you, you who are better than any superiority.
Holy are you, you who surpass any praise.

Accept spiritual, pure sacrifice from (the) soul and (the) heart.
They extend to you, Inexpressible, Unutterable, who can only be named in silence.
Incline to me and empower me, I pray you, not to fall out of the knowledge which corresponds to our nature.

In this grace I will enlighten those who are in ignorance about their origin.
(They are) my brothers, your children.

Therefore I believe and bear witness:
I go to life,
(I go) to light.
You are praised, father.
Your man will hallow with you, because you have given him all power.

The Prayer of the Apostle Paul

The following prayer was unknown before the Nag Hammadi discovery. Formulations like 'psychic God' and 'eternal light-soul' suggest a Gnostic orientation. In form the Prayer of the Apostle Paul (NHC I 1) on the one hand has parallels in the Hermetic writings (e.g. CH XIII 17–20) and on the other recalls the beginning of the Three Steles of Seth (NHC VII 5, see below, pp.89ff.). There are allusions to Old Testament psalms, the Gospel of Philip and to Pauline letters (e.g. I Cor. 2.9).

That the following text is a prayer is clear: first the imperatives as a form of address indicate it, and secondly lines 6–10 have the structure of a hymn. At the beginning of the prayer, each time the petition in the imperative is followed by a divine predication; from line 11 petition and predication are extended by relative clauses. In line 15 a number of petitions without divine predications are put side by side. Here personal statements and christological definitions appear. The last petition is followed by divine predications, a kind of subscript and a liturgical conclusion.

Possibly the Prayer of the Apostle Paul belongs among the prayers which in the context of a sacrament of dying are intended to help the soul of the Gnostic to ascend smoothly past the archons (cf. pp.87ff., Gnostic prayers on dying). Thus the petition for power in line 18 seems to allude to the notion of the ascent of the soul: the Gnostic must be in a position to evade the archons.

[...] [your] light, let me come to your [mercy!
My] Saviour, save me, for [I] belong to you:
[I am] the one who has come forth from you.
You are [my] mind; bring me forth!
You are my treasure house; open for me!
You [are] my fullness; take me to you!
You are (my) repose; give me [the] perfect thing that cannot be grasped!

l beseech you, the one (who you are), the one who is, and the one (who you are), who pre-existed in the name [which is] more exalted than all names, through Jesus Christ, [the Lord] of Lords, the King of the ages;

[give] me your gifts, of which you do not repent, through the Son of Man, [the] Spirit, the Paraclete of [truth].
Give me power, [as I] beseech you!
Give healing for my body, as I ask you through the Evangelist,[38] [and] save my eternal light-soul and my spirit.
And the firstborn of the Pleroma of grace – reveal him to my mind!
Grant what no angel eye has [seen] and no archon ear (has) heard,
and what has not entered into the human heart,
which came into being in an angelic way and (was formed) after the image of the psychic God when it was formed in the beginning!
As I have faith and hope, place upon me your beloved, elect, and praised greatness,
the First-born, the First-begotten,
and the [wonderful] mystery of your house!
[For] yours is the power [and] the glory and the praise and the greatness for ever and ever. [Amen.]

Prayer of Paul (the) Apostle.
In peace. Christ is holy.

The Psalm of Valentinus

The following psalm is one of the oldest pieces of evidence for Gnostic prayer.[39] The psalm, handed down by Hippolytus, is attributed to the Gnostic Valentinus (120–160).[40] The psalm proper is followed by an exegesis and commentary (Hippolytus, *Ref.* VI 37,8), which are probably secondary and were composed by a disciple of Valentinus.

For the psalm, God is an unfathomable depth. One cannot understand or praise God in himself, since no positive statements can be made about him (negative theology). Only through wondering at the work of God, the cosmic order which represents a harmonious, miraculous whole, is it possible to praise God. The positive evaluation of creation, which is unusual for Gnostic thought (but cf. the hymn in CH V), is striking, so that the Gnostic character of this psalm has sometimes been doubted.

The title 'Harvest' is difficult and is a matter of controversy in scholarship. The meaning is probably that the 'harvest of Gnostic knowledge' is being celebrated. This 'spiritual harvest' is possible, as the world is the image of the divine activity.

(Hippolytus, *Ref.* VI 37,7) 'Harvest'
I see how all hangs through spirit,
I understand how all is supported by spirit:
flesh hangs on the soul,
soul hangs on air,
air hangs on the ether.
From a depth fruits arise,
from a womb a child arises.

The Hymns of Attis

The following religious documents were in use among the Naassenes.[41] They are hymns which are addressed to Attis, the deity from Asia Minor. These hymns are not explicitly Gnostic, but they were taken over by the Gnostics and given a Gnostic interpretation.[42] The Christian Gnostics interpreted the biblical text allegorically in order to discover the deep meaning in the text, and treated pagan texts in a similar way:

(Hippolytus, *Ref.* V 9,8)
Be it the race of Kronos,
be it the blessed (child) of Zeus,
be it the (blessed child) of the great Rhea,
hail to Attis, afflicted rumour of Rhea.
The Assyrians call you the thrice-desired Adonis,
all Egypt (calls you) Osiris,
the wisdom of the Greeks (calls you) the heavenly horn of the moon,
the Samothracians (call you) venerable Adamnas,
the Haimonians (call you) Korybas,
the Phrygians (call you) sometimes Papas,
then again corpse or god,

or the one without fear or goatherd, green mown ears,
or the one who bore the many-fruited almond, flute-player.

(Hippolytus, *Ref.* V 9,9) Of Attis will I sing,
the son of Rhea,
not with the sound of bells and not with the flute,
(not) with the trumpeting of Idaean curetes,
but to the muse of Phoebus I make my song ring out:
Jubilation, jubilation! – like Pan, like Bacchus, like a shepherd
of light stars.

2

Fall and Suffering in the World

Precisely how the human soul came to fall or the spark of light left the Pleroma is depicted with different images in the various Gnostic groups. Common to all of them is the result of this fall. The soul is remote from its true origin and in a foreign land. Lulled into a deep sleep by hostile powers and made drunk, it no longer recalls who it really is. Nevertheless it senses its lostness in the world and suffers as a result. Like fallen Sophia (Wisdom), who in the Gnostic images can often no longer be differentiated from the human soul, it laments its suffering and hopes for deliverance from the hostile world. Thus the fate of the soul is one of the central themes in Gnostic literature (cf. the Exegesis of the Soul in the Additional Material; see also the Authentikos Logos [NHC VI 3]).

The fate of the soul among the Mandaeans

The fall of the soul and its deliverance is a central theme among the Mandaeans. Thus for example the whole of the second part of the Ginza, the Left Ginza, deals with the fate of the soul and its ascent on human death. Accordingly the Left Ginza is also called the Mandaean 'Book of the Dead' or 'Book of Souls'.[43] Furthermore the Mandaeans also developed a special 'sacrament of dying', the Masiqta. This is a ceremony which is meant to help the soul in its ascent after death. The Mandaeans composed numerous liturgies within the context of this 'mass of the dead'.[44]

The lament of the soul

(RG XV 9; 322,23ff.) In my mind I contemplate how it happened:
Who took me captive away from my place and my abode, from the circle of my parents who brought me up?

Who brought me to the guilty ones, the sons of the dwelling which is nothingness?
Who brought me to the rebels who wage war daily?
Who showed me the bitterness in which is no sweetness?
Who showed me the darkness in which there is no ray of light?
Who showed me the stinking water that turns on wheels?

(LG III 42; 119,21f.) Who threw me into the Tibil (= the earthly world)?
Into the Tibil who threw me?
Who shut me up in the wall?
Who threw me into the stocks which are like the fullness of the worlds?
Who put a chain around me which is beyond measure?
Who clothed me with a garment of all colours and kinds?[45]

From the Mandaean mass of the dead

The following evidence for Mandaean piety has its *Sitz im Leben* in the Mandaean Mass of the Dead (Masiqta). It expresses the fate of the soul in the body, but also the state of the liberated soul. There is also a polemical attitude towards the 'Former of Bodies'. This motif is attested in many Gnostic writings in the form of polemic against the demiurge.

(ML 69) May peace and welfare prevail on the way which Adam rightly built.
May peace and welfare prevail on the way which the soul takes.

The soul loosed the chain, she shattered the fetters.
She shed the bodily garment.
She turned round, saw it and quaked.
She uttered an evil curse on the man who clothed her with the body.
She provoked the Former of Bodies and roused him from the place in which he lay.
She said to him, 'Rise up, look, you Former of Bodies, the hollows of your hands are filling with water!'

The voice of the Former of Bodies it is that weeps and laments about himself.
He says, 'Woe is me that the hollows of my hands
are filled with water!'
To her (viz., the soul), he says:
'Go in peace, you nobly born, whom they have called a servant in the abode of the evil ones.
Go in peace, you pure pearl, you who were taken from the treasury of life.
Go in peace, you light-giving one, you who lightened the dark house.
Go in peace, elect, pure one, sinless without a flaw!'

The soul flies and goes until she comes to the house of life:
When she came to the house of life, the powers[46] came to meet her.
They said to her, 'Take and put on your robe of radiance and lay upon yourself your magnificent garland.
Arise, dwell in the heavenly places,[47] the place in which the powers dwell.'[48]
Life is upheld and is victorious, and victorious is Manda-dHaije and those who love his name. And praised be life![49]

The fate of the soul among the Manichaeans

In Manichaean mythology, too, the soul is part of the primal human being and thus a part of the world of light. It is imprisoned in the body, which belongs to the darkness-world.

Manichaean psalm to the soul

The following Manichaean psalm sings of the calamitous situation of the soul in the world and at the same time contains an invitation to the soul to recall her true homeland.

(MPB II 181,19ff.) Soul, soul, be mindful of your aeons.
(*The words 'be mindful [of your aeons]' are repeated as a refrain after each line.*)

O soul, where do you come from?
You come from on high.
You are a stranger to the world,
a visitor on the earth [of] human beings.
You have your houses on high,
your tents of joy.
You have your true father,
your true mother.
You have your true brothers.
You are a warrior.
You are the sheep
that went astray in the wilderness.
Your father is seeking you,
your shepherd is searching for your sake.
You are the vine,
the (one) with five branches,
which you become for the food of the gods,
for the nourishment of the angels,
for the clothing of the righteous,
for the robe of the holy,
which you become for the mind of the perfect,
for the thought of the believers.
Soul, raise yourself
in this house which is full of (mourning).
[...] demons,
[...] of robbers.
Soul, do not forget yourself.
For they are all hunting for you.
They are all hunting for you,
the hunters of death.
They catch the birds.
[...]
They [break] their [wings],
so that they cannot fly to their nests.
Soul, raise yourself
and go to your fatherland.
You are a stranger to your kin.
[Go into the house] full of joy.

You [...] light
from everlasting to everlasting.
Praise and honour be to Jesus, the king of the holy ones!
Victory be to the soul of the blessed Mary.[50]

Manichaean dialogue between the soul and the Saviour

Like the first psalm, the following Manichaean psalm is one of the
'Psalms of the Wanderer'. In form it represents a cultic dialogue
between the soul in tribulation and its Saviour. The soul imprisoned
in the body asks how it is to attain to real life. The psalm essentially
consists in the Saviour's answer. To the invitation is attached the
positive formulation of the soul's question as a refrain ('My soul, and
you [shall live]'). Such liturgical dialogues between the Saviour and the
soul, the child or the body can often be found in Manichaean texts (cf.
M 42; PsTh 14).[51]

(MPB II 182,20–183,18). (*The soul asks*): 'What shall I do that
I may live?
My Redeemer, what shall I do that I may live?'
(*Jesus answers*:) 'Continue with your fasting, my soul, and you
shall live!
Give rest to your hands!
Clothe yourself with the purity of the truth!
Give love (to your) mind!
(Give) faith to your thought!
(Give) perfection (to your) instruction!
(Give) perseverance (to your) plan!
(Give) wisdom (to your) reflection!
Give room to the doves,
those with the white wings.
Let them dwell among you
and [...] before your face.
Let no serpent to [them]
so that they are not afraid of you.
[...]
[...] mourning [...].
Give no room to anger!

Humble (your) desire!
Keep (false) busyness in check!
Do not disseminate teaching [...]!
Love of God,
faith in the commandment,
perfection do you perfect,
perseverance do you persevere.
Know in order to grasp it!
Keep the commandments!
Perfect the works!
Remain [...]
from eternity to eternity!
Victory to the soul of the blessed Mary![52]

The Pistis Sophia psalms

The Pistis Sophia is a Gnostic writing from the third century and in form is conceived as a dialogue between the Risen Christ and his disciples, women and men. It consists of four books in all, the fourth of which was probably originally independent.[53] The Pistis Sophia writings are among the most comprehensive testimonies of Gnostics to themselves and are close to Barbelo Gnosticism.

In content the Pistis Sophia is a very complex work: sacraments, magic, descriptions of the heavenly regions which also appear in the Untitled text in the Bruce Codex are represented. Central, however, is the fate of Pistis Sophia (chs. 32ff.). Pistis Sophia longs for the world of light above. As a consequence of her longing she is entangled in matter. She sends thirteen penitential prayers in all to the light above. After the ninth penitential prayer Jesus is sent into the chaotic world at the command of the First Mystery to save Pistis Sophia. The penitential prayers of Pistis Sophia are followed by prayers of thanksgiving for her deliverance (see below). In connection with the fate of Pistis Sophia, Jesus depicts his journey through the aeons and his ascent past the archons.

The fate of Pistis Sophia is to be identified with the fate of the human soul generally. To this degree the lamentations and penitential prayers of Pistis Sophia reflect the repentance of the human soul and its need for salvation. In form, the penitential prayers are spoken by the Risen Christ. The hymns are followed by 'interpretations' of them by the disciples of Jesus, women and men. Both Old Testament psalms and Odes of Solomon[54] are used in depicting the fate of Pistis Sophia.

Psalm of lamentation 1

(Chapter 32) Light of lights, in whom I have believed from the beginning,
hear now, light, my repentance.
Deliver me, light, for wicked thoughts have entered into me.
I looked, O light, to the parts below; I saw a light there;
I thought: I will go to that place to take that light.
And I went; I came to be in the darkness which prevails in the chaos below, and I could not rush out and go to my place,
because I was oppressed among all the emanations of the Authades,[55]
and the lion-faced power took away my light which was in me.
And I cried for help,
and my voice did not penetrate out of the darkness,
and I looked to the height,
so that the Light in which I had believed might come to my help.
And when I looked to the height, I saw all the archons of the aeons:
they were numerous and they looked down upon me and rejoiced over me;
I had done nothing evil to them, but they hated me without cause.
And when the emanations of the Authades saw that the archons of the aeons were rejoicing over me,
they knew that the archons of the aeons would not come to my help.
And those emanations which oppressed me with violence took courage:
and they took from me the light which I did not take from them.
Now at this time, true Light – you know that I have done these things in my innocence;

I thought that the lion-faced light belonged to you,
and the sin which I have committed is manifest to you.

Do not let me be lacking, Lord,
for I have believed in your light from the beginning, Lord,
light of the powers;
do not let me lack my light.

For at your instigation and because of your light I have come to
be in this oppression; and shame has covered me.

And because of your light[56] I have become a stranger to my
brothers, the invisible ones, and also (to) the great emanations
of the Barbelo.

These things happened to me, Light, because I longed for your
dwelling-place,
and the anger of the Authades came down upon me
– this one who did not obey your command to emanate from
the emanation of his power –
because I was in his aeon without performing his mystery.
And all the archons of the aeons mocked me.
And I was in that place,
mourning and seeking the light
which I had seen in the height.
And the watchers of the gates of the aeons were seeking me,
and all those who continued in their mystery mocked me.
But I looked up to the height to you, light, and believed in you.
Now at this time, light of lights, I am oppressed in the darkness
of the chaos.
If now you want to come to save me
– great is your mercy –
hear me truly and save me.
Save me out of the matter of this darkness,
so that I shall not be submerged in it,
so that I shall be delivered from the emanations of the divine
Authades which oppress me, and from their evils!
Do not let this darkness submerge me,

and do not let this lion-faced power swallow up all my power completely,
and do not let this Chaos cover over my power.
Hear me, Light, for your mercy is precious,
and look down upon me according to the great mercy of your light.
Do not turn away your face from me, for I am greatly tormented.
Hear me immediately and save my power.
Save me, on account of the archons which hate me,
for you know my oppression and my torment and the torment of my power
which they have taken from me.
Those who have planted me in all this evil are in your presence; deal with them according to your pleasure.

My power looked forth from the midst of the Chaos and the midst of the darknesses,
and I looked for my pair,[57] that he would come and fight for me;
and he did not come, and I expected that he would come and give me strength, and I did not find him.
And when I sought the light, they gave me darkness,
and when I sought my power, they gave me matter.
Now at this time, light of lights, let the darkness and the matter which the emanations of the Authades have brought upon me become a snare for them, and let them be ensnared in it.
May you repay them and may they know scandal, and not come to the place of their Authades.
Let them remain in darkness and not see the light.
Let them look at the chaos at all times.
And let them not look at the height.
Bring their vengeance upon them, and may your judgment seize them.
Do not let them go to their place from now on, to their divine Authades,
and do not let his emanations come to their places from now on, for their god is godless and complacent.

And he thought that he had done this evil by himself;
he did not know that he would have had no power over me,
had I not been humbled according to your ordinance.
But when you had humbled me through your ordinance,
they persecuted me all the more,
and their emanations have inflicted torments upon my humiliation.
And they have taken a light-power from me and again begun to
torment me greatly, in order to take away all the light that was
in me.
Because of the things into which they have planted me,
do not let them go up to the thirteenth aeon, the place of righteousness.
And do not let them be reckoned within the portion of those
who purify themselves and their light;
and do not let them be reckoned among those who will feel
repentance immediately,
so that they immediately receive mysteries in the light.

For they have taken my light from me,
and my power is beginning to fail within me,
and I have lack in my light.

Now at this time, light, which is in you and is with me,
I praise your name, light in glory.
And may my song of praise please you, light, like an excellent
mystery which leads into the gates of light,
which those who feel repentance may speak and whose light
they will purify.
Now at this time may all material things rejoice;
Seek the light, all of you, that the power of your souls which is
in you may live.
For the light has heard the material things and will not leave any
material thing,
without having purified it.
Let the souls and the material things bless the Lord of all the
aeons,
and the material things and all that are in them.

For God will save their souls from all material things,
and a city will be prepared in the light,
and all souls which will be redeemed will dwell in that city and
will inherit it.
And the soul of those who will receive mysteries will abide in
that place,
and those who have received mysteries in his name will abide in
it.

Psalm of lamentation 5

(Chapter 41) Light of my deliverance, I sing praise to you in the
place of the height, and again in the chaos.
I will sing praise to you in my song, with which I have praised
you in the height, and with which I have praised you when I was
in the chaos. May it reach you! And heed, light, my repentance.

My power has filled itself with darkness; and my light has come
down into the chaos.
I myself have become like the archons of the chaos which have
gone to the lower darkness. I have become like a material body,
which has no one in the height who will deliver it.
I have become like material things whose power has been taken
from them as they were cast into the chaos, which you have not
delivered; and they have been destroyed by your ordinance.

Now at this time I have been placed in the lower darkness, in
dark things and in material things which are dead. And there is
no power in them.
You have brought your ordinance upon me with all things
which you have ordained.
And the Spirit has departed; it has left me. And again – through
your ordinance the emanations of my aeon have not helped me.
And they have hated me and abandoned me; and yet I am not
completely destroyed.
And my light has diminished in me. And I have cried out to the

light with all the light that is in me.
And I have stretched out my hands to you.
(...)

And I have sung praise to you, light, and my repentance will
reach you in the height.
May your light come down upon me.
My light has been taken from me, and I am suffering because of
the light, from the time when I was sent forth. And when I
looked into the height at the light, I looked down on the light-
power which is in the chaos.
I stood up; I came down.
Your ordinance has come upon me, and the anguishes which
you ordained for me have shaken me.
And they surrounded me like roaring water, they seized me all
at once for all time.
And through your ordinance you have not allowed those who
have been sent forth with me to help me; and you have not
allowed my pair to deliver me from my sufferings.

The Naassene Psalm

A hymn of the soul has been preserved by the church father Hippolytus
(beginning of the third century) which is attributed to the Naassene
Gnostics (see n.41). Unfortunately the text of this hymn is badly
damaged.[58] Although the psalm is attributed to a specific Gnostic
group, it is commonplace Gnostic material; it contains many Gnostic
key words (chaos, seal, way, mystery, knowledge). Central to it is the
notion of the ascent of the soul and connected with that its salvation
from matter: Gnosis is the knowledge of the way communicated by the
Gnostic Saviour, which leads from the material world, felt to be
negative, to the heavenly home. This notion is determinative for
Gnostic thought[59] (cf. simply the Gnostic catechisms and in general the
sacrament of dying).

The Naassene Psalm can be regarded as a compendium and
summary of the Gnostic doctrine of salvation generally. Formally the
hymn consists of two parts: the first part is a poetic expression of the

fate of the soul and its sufferings in the world. The second part describes the action of the Saviour, who seeks to deliver the soul from its hopeless situation.

(Hippolytus, *Ref.* V 10,2)
The universal law of all was the first-born mind,
the second was the chaos, which was poured out by the first-born.
But third the soul received a real law.
Therefore she is wrapped in a fleeting form.
She toils, driven by the fear of death.
Sometimes she has the mastery and sees the light.
Sometimes she is hurled out into the cave and weeps.
Sometimes she rejoices, sometimes she will bewail.
Sometimes she condemns, sometimes she will be condemned.
Sometimes she dies, sometimes she arises.[60]
Unfortunate one, she no longer knows any way out.
Wandering she runs into a labyrinth.

Then said Jesus, 'Behold, Father!
As a prey of evil she roams over the earth,
away from your breath.
She attempts to escape the bitter chaos,
and does not know how to get through it.

Therefore send me, Father!
With seals (in my hand) I will descend.
I will pass through all aeons,
all mysteries I will unveil,
the forms of the gods I will show,
and the hidden things of the holy way which I call Gnosis will I hand over.'

From the Exegesis of the Soul

The Exegesis of the Soul (see Additional Material) contains a prayer which is about the repentance of the soul over its fall.[61]

(NHC II 6; 135,4ff.) It is therefore fitting to pray to the Father and to call on him with all our soul – not (only) outwardly with the lips, but with the spirit, which is inward, which came forth from the depth:

we sigh,
we repent of the life that we lived,
we confess our sins,
we perceive the vain deception we were in,
and the vain zeal;
we weep over how we were in darkness and in the wave,[62]
we mourn for ourselves, that he may have pity on us;
we hate ourselves as we now are.

From the Books of Jeu

The two Books of Jeu[63] belong to the same group of Gnostic writings as the Pistis Sophia and the Untitled Text, which contains a description of heaven. Like the Pistis Sophia, the two Books of Jeu are revelation dialogues in which Jesus communicates to his disciples mysteries from the world above. In them the sacramental (see below) and magical character of particular Gnostic tendencies emerges. Three fragments have been handed down in the Books of Jeu. Two of them are Gnostic prayers for a hearing. It is impossible to discover with any certainty who is praying and to whom the prayer in Fragment 1 is addressed, but Fragment 2 does allow us to draw some conclusions: the notion that all the sparks of light which have been lost and dispersed in matter have to be collected before the complete restoration of the Pleroma takes place is frequently attested in Gnostic texts (see also the introduction to the bridal hymn from the Acts of Thomas, see below, p.101). Since the suppliant speaks of 'his members' which have been dispersed and must be gathered together, it seems likely that the person praying in this hymn is referring to the Gnostic Saviour figure.[64]

What is striking in both fragments is the constant repetition of particular formulations almost in a solemn monotone; in Fragment 2 even the texts of different sections of the prayer are completely equal; only the heavenly spheres vary. The magic names customary in Gnosticism, which serve as invocations and have magical power, are also very important here (cf. also the baptismal prayer from the Gospel of the Egyptians, below, p.95).

Fragment of a Gnostic hymn I

(pp.87ff. [2 Jeu]) Hear me – I sing your praise, O mystery, (you) who existed before any incomprehensible one and (before) any unlimited one.

Hear me – I sing your praise, O mystery, (you) who have shone in your mystery, so that the mystery which exists from the beginning will be fulfilled! And (when you) shone, (you became) water of the ocean, *your*[65] *imperishable name is aezōa.*

Hear me – I sing your praise, O mystery, (you) who existed before every incomprehensible one, and (before) every unlimited one, (you) who have shone in your mystery. The earth in the midst of the ocean was purified, *your* *imperishable name is azōae.*

Hear me – I sing your praise, O mystery, (you) who existed before every incomprehensible one and (before) every unlimited one, (you) who have shone in your mystery. The whole powerful matter of the ocean, which is the sea, was purified together with all the forms in it, *your imperishable name is aozoa.*

Hear me – I sing your praise, O mystery, (you) who existed before every incomprehensible one and (before) every unlimited one, (you) who have shone in your mystery. And (when you) shone, (you) sealed the sea together with all that is in it, for the force in it was in disorder, *your imperishable name [is] [...]*

Hear me – I sing your praise, O mystery, (you) who existed before [every incomprehensible one] [...]

Fragment of a Gnostic hymn II

(pp.35ff. [1 Jeu]) *Hear me – I sing your praise, O first mystery, (you) who have shone in your mystery, (you) who have caused Jeu to establish the fifth aeon;[66] and you have instituted archons, decans[67] and ministers* in the fifth aeon, *whose imperishable name is psamazaz.* Save all my members which have been scattered since the foundation of the world in all the archons and the decans and the ministers of the fifth aeon; and gather them all together and take them into the light.

Hear me – I sing your praise, O first mystery, (you) who have shone in your mystery, (you) who have caused Jeu to establish the sixth aeon; and you have instituted archons, decans and ministers in the sixth aeon, *whose imperishable name is zaouza.* Save all my members which have been scattered since the foundation of the world in the archons and the decans and the ministers of the sixth aeon; gather them all together and take them into the light.

Hear me – I sing your praise, O first mystery, (you) who have shone in your mystery, (you) who have caused Jeu to establish the seventh aeon; and you have instituted archons, decans and ministers in the seventh aeon, *whose imperishable name is chazabraōza.* Save all my members which have been scattered since the foundation of the world in the archons and the decans and the ministers of the seventh aeon; gather them all together and take them into the light.

Hear me – I sing your praise, O first mystery, (you) who have shone in your mystery, (you) who have caused Jeu to establish the eighth aeon; and you have founded archons, decans and ministers in the eighth aeon, *whose imperishable name is banaza* ... Save all my members which have been scattered since the foundation of the world in all the archons and the decans and the ministers of the eighth aeon; gather them all together and take them into the light.

Hear me – I sing your praise, O first mystery, (you) who have shone in your mystery, (you) who have caused Jeu to establish the ninth aeon; and you have instituted archons, decans and ministers in the ninth aeon, *whose imperishable name is dazaōza.* Save all my members which have been scattered since the foundation (of the world) in the archons and the decans and the ministers of the ninth aeon; gather them all together and take them into the light.

Hear me – I sing your praise, O first mystery, (you) who have shone in your mystery, (you) who have caused Jeu to establish the tenth aeon; and you have instituted archons, decans and ministers in the tenth aeon, *whose imperishable name is tanouaz.* Save all my members which have been scattered since the foundation of the world in all the archons and the decans and the ministers of the tenth aeon; gather them all together and take them into the light.

Hear me – I sing your praise, O first mystery, (you) who have shone in your mystery, (you) who have caused Jeu to establish the eleventh aeon; and you have instituted archons, decans and ministers in the eleventh aeon, *whose imperishable name is plouzaaa.* Save all my members which have been scattered since the foundation of the world in all the archons and the decans and the ministers of the eleventh aeon; gather them all together and take them into the Light.

Hear me – I sing your praise, O first mystery, (you) who have shone in your mystery, (you) who have caused Jeu to establish the twelfth aeon; and you have instituted archons, decans and ministers in the twelfth aeon, *whose imperishable name is parnaza.* Save all my members which have been scattered since the foundation of the world in all the archons and the decans and the ministers of the twelfth aeon; gather them all together and take them into the light.

Hear me – I sing your praise, O first mystery, (you) who have shone in your mystery, (you) who have caused Jeu to establish the place of the twenty-four invisible emanations, with their archons and their gods and their lords and their archangels and their angels and their decans and their ministers, in an ordinance of the thirteenth aeon, *whose imperishable name is ōazanazaō.* Save all my members which have been scattered since the foundation of the world in the twenty-four invisible emanations and their archons and their gods and their lords and their archangels and their angels and their decans and their ministers; and gather them all together and take them into the light.

Hear me – I sing your praise, O first mystery, (you) who have shone in your mystery, (you) who have caused Jeu to establish the thirteenth aeon; and you have instituted three gods and the invisible one in the thirteenth aeon, *whose imperishable name is Iazazaaa*. Save all my members which have been scattered in the three gods and the invisible one; and gather them all together and take them into the light.

Hear me – I sing your praise, O first mystery, (you) who have shone in your mystery and have established all the archons together with Jabraoth, who have believed in the kingdom of light, in a place of pure air, *whose imperishable name is chachazaōraza*. Save all my members which have been scattered since the foundation of the world in all the archons and the decans and the ministers; and gather them all together and take them all into the light. Amen, Amen.

3

Salvation and Return

The salvation of the self is the topic of most Gnostic prayers and hymns. Salvation takes place through knowledge of one's own origin, which is communicated by the Gnostic saviour figure. Thus many liturgical texts deal with the saviour figure and its work.[68] Here the origin of numerous documents is to be directly associated with the Gnostic sacraments, through which salvation is communicated to the Gnostics.

The discussion about the status of cult and liturgy in Gnosticism has a long history. The sacramental character of Gnosticism has been denied completely, and it has been regarded as a philosophy of religion;[69] Gnosticism has also been put among the mystery associations.[70] Though we cannot go into this discussion in detail here,[71] it should be pointed out that as a result of the Nag Hammadi discovery there are new indications of the cultic character of Gnostic and Hermetic communities (cf. only the Gospel of Philip [NHC II 3] and the Three Steles of Seth [NHC VII 5]).[72]

'I am' hymns of saviour figures

The deliverance of the Gnostic self imprisoned in the world takes place through its coming to know its true origin, from which it has been alienated. This knowledge is communicated to it by the saviour figure. Therefore numerous hymns depict the work of the Gnostic saviour figure. Most of these texts are composed in the first-person, 'I am', style (cf. also Second Apocalypse of James [NHC V 4; 48, 1ff.]) which is matched by a 'You are' or 'He is' from the answering community.

From the Sophia Jesu Christi

The Sophia Jesu Christi is a didactic dialogue between Jesus and his disciples. This writing has a multiple tradition: one version is in the

Nag Hammadi library (NHC III 4), another is in the Berlin Codex (BG
8502, 2). It is based on a work which is a letter by a Gnostic teacher
called Eugnostos; the content of this letter is not of Christian origin (cf.
above, p.17). The insertion of the Christian dialogue partner has transformed this letter into a Christian-Gnostic revelation dialogue. In
addition to the insertion of the narrative framework, the Sophia Jesu
Christi also contains Gnostic Christian special material which
describes above all the origin and activity of the Saviour. This includes
revelations from the mouth of Christ which take the form of 'I am'
predications. The following text is based on the version from the Nag
Hammadi library (NHC III 4); text that is missing from that has been
supplied from the Berlin Codex version (BG).

(NHC III 4; 107,11,11ff.) But I, I came from the places above
by the will of the great light,
I who had got free from that bond.
I have cut off the work of the robbers.
I have awakened that drop that was sent by Sophia,
that it might bear much fruit through me and be perfected and
no longer be defective, but be joined through me, the great
Saviour,
that his glory might be revealed,
so that Sophia might also be acquitted of that defect,
so that her sons might no longer be defective, but receive
honour and glory and go up to their Father and know the words
of the masculine Light.

(BG 121,13ff.) Now I have taught you about the immortal
human being.
And I have loosed the fetters of the robbers from him.
I have shattered the gates of the merciless ones before their face.
I have humiliated their pronoia. They have all been put to
shame and they have risen from their forgetfulness.
That is indeed why I have come here,
that they might be joined with this spirit (NHC III 4; 117,1ff.)
and breath and from two might become one as from the
beginning,
that you might yield abundant fruit and go up to Him Who Is

from the beginning, in inexpressible joy and glory and [honour and] grace of the [Father of the All].
(...)
Behold, I have revealed to you the name of the Perfect One,
the whole will of the mother of the holy angels,
that the [masculine multitude] might be completed here,
that [the infinities might be made manifest in the aeons and] those who [arose in the] untraceable [wealth of the Great] invisible [Spirit, that they] all [might take from his goodness] even the wealth [of their rest], which has no [kingdom over it].
I came [from the First], (the one) who has been sent, that I might reveal to you Him Who Is from the beginning, because of the arrogance of the First-Begetter and his angels.
(...)
Now I have come to lead them out of their blindness, that I might report to each about God who is above the All. Therefore, trample on their graves, suppress their pronoia and shatter their yoke and establish my own.
I have given you authority over all things as sons of light, that you might tread upon their power with your feet.

From the Apocryphon of John

In the Apocryphon of John, too, at the end of the revelation there is a hymn in which the saviour figure describes his activity. Here the multiple descent of the saviour figure, which is often attested in Gnostic texts, is striking (cf. the Paraphrase of Shem [NHC VII 1]; the 'Trimorphic Protennoia' [NHC XIII 1]).[73]

(NHC II 1; 30,11ff.) Now I, the perfect pronoia of the All, changed myself into my seed,
for I was (present) first, and went on every way.
For I am the richness of the light, I am the thought of the Pleroma.
And I went to the magnitude of darkness and I endured
until I entered the middle of the prison.
And the foundations of chaos were shaken.

And I, I hid myself from them because of their wickedness,
and they did not recognize me.
Again I returned for the second time.
I went,
I came forth from those who belong to the light,
– that is what I am – the thought of the pronoia.
I went into the midst of darkness and into the inside of the
underworld.[74]
I wanted (to accomplish) my task.
And the foundations of chaos were shaken,
so that they might fall upon those who are in chaos and destroy
them.
And again I ran up to my root of light,
so that they will not be destroyed before the time.
Furthermore, for the third time I went
– I am the light which exists in the light, I am the thought of the
pronoia –
so that I might enter into the midst of darkness and the inside
of the underworld.
And I filled my face with the light of the completion of their
aeon.
And I entered into the midst of their prison
which is the prison *of the* body.
(*There follows a section on the awakening call, see above, p.80*).

Bronte

Bronte (NHC VI 2) is one of the hymnic texts from Nag Hammadi and
consists of a self-predication of a figure which unites all opposites in
itself.[75] Such an 'I am' discourse occurs often in Nag Hammadi texts
(see e.g. the Trimorphic Protennoia [NHC XIII 1]) and throughout
antiquity (cf. the Isis aretalogy of Kyme; Sir. 24).

   What is striking about Bronte is the antithetical way in which the
self-predicates are carried through, which shows similarities to the
Christ hymn of the Acts of John (94–96, see below, pp.67ff.).[76] These
oppositions in what the revealer figures say of themselves are probably
an echo of ancient riddle literature. Knowledge (and the deciphering
associated with it) of the revealer figures brings salvation. If human

beings awaken and become sober, they hasten to their place of rest and there find rest and immortality. Thus the last page of Bronte is also the key to the interpretation of the whole text: 'And they will find me there, and they will live, and they will not die again' (21, 24ff.). The numerous promises and admonitions in Bronte can also be understood from this point: listening to the revealer and entering into a relationship with her is a presupposition for knowing her. The revealer figure in Bronte admonishes this at many points.

Scholars have long puzzled over the title Bronte (= Thunder). However, we may assume that 'thunder' is to be understood in terms of the heavenly voice of Athena-Sophia (M. Tardieu). The introduction of a heavenly voice as a revealer figure is also attested in Gnosticism (cf. e.g. the Letter of Peter to Philip [NHC VIII 2; 134,14ff.]; Epiphanius, *Haer.* 26,3,1 see n.64).

It cannot be established with certainty whether Bronte has a clearly Jewish, Christian or Gnostic character, but at all events it has been stamped by wisdom. There are close connections with Wisdom 7.22ff. and Sir. 24 in particular.

(NHC VI 2; 13, 1ff.) The Thunder: The Perfect Mind.
I was sent forth from [the] power.
And I have come to those who think about me.
And I have been found among those who seek after me.
Look upon me, you who think about me!
And you hearers, hear me!
You who are waiting for me, take me to yourselves!
And do not banish me from your sight!
And do not make your voice hate me nor your hearing!
Do not be ignorant of me anywhere or any time!
Be on your guard!
Do not be ignorant of me!

For I am the first and the last.
I am the honoured one and the despised one.
I am the whore and the holy one.
I am the wife and the virgin.
I am *the mother* and the daughter.
I am the members of my mother.
I am the barren one, and many are her sons.

I am she whose wedding(s) are numerous, and I have not taken a husband.
I am the midwife and she who does not bear.
I am the comfort of my labour pains.
I am the bride and the bridegroom.
And it is my husband who brought me forth.
I am the mother of my father and the sister of my husband, and he (viz. husband) is my offspring.
I am the slave of him who prepared me.
I am the ruler of my offspring.
But he (viz., the Father) is the one who [begot me] before the time,
on a day of birth.
And he is my offspring [in] (due) time,
and my power stems from him.
I am the staff of his power in his youth,
[and] he is the support of my old age.
And whatever he wills, that happens to me.

I am the silence that is unattainable
and the thought whose remembrance is frequent.
I am the voice whose sound is manifold
and the word whose appearance
is multiple.
I am the utterance of my name.

Why do you love me, you who hate me,
and hate those who love me?
You who deny me, confess me,
and you who confess me, deny me!
You who tell the truth about me, spread lies about me!
And you who have spread lies about me, tell the truth about me!
You who know me, be ignorant of me,
and let those who have not known me, know me!

For I am knowledge and ignorance.
I am shame and free speech.
I am shameless; I am ashamed.

I am strength and I am fear.
I am war and peace.
Give heed to me.
I am the one who is scorned and (I am) the great one.

Give heed to my poverty and my wealth.
Do not be arrogant to me when I am cast upon the earth,
[and] you will find me in [those who] come.
And do not look (down) [upon] me on the dungheap,
and do not abandon me when I am cast out,
and you will find me in the kingdoms.
Do not look (down) upon me
when I am thrown among those who are scorned and in the
lowliest places.
And do not laugh at me.
And do not cast me down to those who have a defect in (their)
hard-heartedness.
But I, I am merciful, and I am cruel.

Be on your guard!
Do not hate my obedience and do not love my continence.
In my weakness, do not forsake me.
And do not be afraid of my power.
For why do you despise my fear and curse my pride?
But I am she who is in every fear,
and strength in trembling.
I am she who is weak,
and I am unharmed in a place of joy.
I am without understanding,
and I am wise.

Why have you hated me in your counsels?
For I shall be silent among those who are silent.
And I shall appear and speak.
Why now have you hated me, you Greeks?
Because I am a barbarian among [the] Barbarians?
For I am the wisdom [of the] Greeks
and the knowledge [of the] Barbarians.

I am judgment [for the] Greeks and the Barbarians.
[I] am the one whose image is great in Egypt
and the one who has no image among the Barbarians.
I am the one who has been hated everywhere,
and the one who has been loved everywhere.
I am the one who is called 'Life',
and you have called me 'Death'.
I am the one who is called 'Law',
and you have called me 'Lawlessness'.
I am the one whom you have pursued,
and I am the one whom you have seized.
I am the one whom you have scattered,
and you have gathered me together.
I am the one before whom you have been ashamed,
and you have been shameless to me.
I am the one who does not hold festivals,
and I am the one whose festivals are many.
I, I am godless, and
I am the one whose God is great.
I am the one on whom you have thought,
and you have despised me.
I am without wisdom,
and they learn from me.
I am the one for whom you have contempt,
and you think about me.

I am the one from whom you have hidden,
and you appear to me.
Now when you hide yourselves, I will reveal myself.
For [when] you [appear],
I myself [will hide] from you.
(...)
Why do you curse me
and honour me?
You have wounded (me)
and you have had mercy (on me).
(...)
But I am the mind of [...] and the rest of [...].

I am the knowledge of my enquiry,
and the finding of those who seek after me,
and the command of those who ask of me,
and the power of the powers in my knowledge of the angels,
who have been sent out at my word,
and of the gods among the gods through my counsel,
and of spirits of every man who is in me,
and of every woman who is in me.

I am the one who is honoured, and the one who is praised,
and the one who is scornfully held in contempt.
I am peace,
and war has arisen because of me.
And I am an alien and a citizen.
I am the substance and the one who is without substance.
Those who come from my company do not know me,
and those who are in my substance know me.
Those who are close to me did not know me,
and those who are far away from me are the ones who have
known me.
On the day when I am close [to you], I am far [from you],
and on the day when I [am far] from you, [I am close] to you.
(...)
[I am] the graspable and the ungraspable.
I am the union and the dissolution.
I am the abiding and I am the dissolving.[77]
I am the one below, and they will come up to me.
I am the condemnation and the acquittal.
I, I am sinless, and the root of sin derives from me.

I am lust in appearance,
and continence of the heart is in me.
I am the hearing which is attainable to everyone
and the speech which cannot be grasped.
I am a mute who does not speak,
and great is the number of my words.

Hear me in gentleness, and receive teaching of me in harshness.
I am she who cries out,

and I am cast upon the face of the earth.
I prepare the bread and my mind within.
I am the knowledge of my name.
I am the one who cries out, and I listen.
(...)
You honour me (...) and you whisper against [me].
You [who] are vanquished, judge those (who vanquish you) before they give judgment against you, for the judge and regard exist in you.
If you are condemned by this one, who will acquit you?
Or if you are acquitted by him, who will be able to seize you?

Your inside is your outside.
And the one who fashions your outside is the one who has shaped your inside.
And what you see outside you, you see inside you.
It is manifest, and it is your garment.

Hear me, you hearers, and learn from my words, you who know me.
I am the hearing that is attainable in every respect.
I am the speech that cannot be grasped.
I am the name of the sound and the sound of the name.
I am the sign of the letter and the manifestation of the division.
(...)
Look now at his words and all the writings which have been fulfilled.
Give heed, you hearers, and you also, angels, and those who have been sent, and you spirits who have risen from the dead.
For I am the one who alone exists.
And I have no one who will judge me.

For many are the pleasant forms which are in numerous sins, and incontinencies, and scorned passions, and fleeting pleasures, which hold (human beings) fast, until they become sober and hasten up to their resting-place.

And they will find me there, and they will live, and they will not die again.

A Christ hymn from the Acts of John

Together with the revelation discourse about the mystery of the cross
(87–105), this dance hymn of Christ belongs among the pieces of
Gnostic tradition in the Acts of John, an apocryphal collection of
actions by the apostle John from the second or third century CE. The
liturgical *Sitz im Leben* of the Christ hymn could lie in a Gnostic
(Valentinian) dedication ritual.[78] A similar ritual in which the disciples
respond to praises of Jesus with 'Amen' also appears in the First Book
of Jeu (see pp.26f.). This unique text has regularly been set to music
and developed in literary form right down to the present day.[79]

(Acts of John 94–96) So he told us to form a circle, holding one
another's hands, and himself stood in the middle and said,
'Answer "Amen" to me.'
So he began to sing a hymn and to say, 'Glory be to you,
Father.'
And we circled round him and answered him, 'Amen.'

'Glory be to you, Word:
Glory be to you, Grace.' – 'Amen.'
'Glory be to you, Spirit:
Glory be to you, Holy One.
Glory be to you in glory.' – 'Amen.'
'We praise you, Father:
We thank you, Light:
In whom darkness does not dwell.' – 'Amen.'

'And why we give thanks, I say:
I want to be saved,
and I want to save.' – 'Amen.'
'I want to be redeemed,
and I want to redeem.' – 'Amen.'
'I want to be wounded,
and I want to wound.' – 'Amen.'
'I want to be begotten,
and I want to beget.' – 'Amen.'
'I want to eat,
and I want to be fed.' – 'Amen.'

'I want to hear,
and I want to be heard.' – 'Amen.'
'I want to be understood,
I who am fully understanding.' – 'Amen.'
'I want to be washed,
and I want to wash.' – 'Amen.'

'Grace dances.
I want to pipe,
tread a measure, all of you.' – 'Amen.'
'I want to begin a mourning song,
mourn, all.' – 'Amen.'
'(The) one Eighth
sings praises with us.' – 'Amen.'
'The twelfth number
dances on high.' – 'Amen.'
'To the All
it belongs to dance.' (?) – 'Amen.'
'He who does not dance, does not know
what happens.' – 'Amen.'

'I want to flee,
and I want to remain.' – 'Amen.'
'I want to equip,
and I want to be equipped.' – 'Amen.'
'I want to be united,
and I want to unite.' – 'Amen.'
'I have no house,
and I have houses.' – 'Amen.'
'I have no place,
and I have places.' – 'Amen.'
'I have no temple
and I have temples.' – 'Amen.'
'I am a lamp to you
who see me.' – 'Amen.'
'I am a mirror to you
who understand me.' – 'Amen.'
'I am a door to you

who knock on me.' – 'Amen.'
'I am a way to you
who travel.' – ('Amen')

'Follow my dance,
see yourself in me, I am speaking,
and when you have seen what I do,
keep silence about my mysteries.
You who dance, understand
what I do, for yours is
this human suffering,
which I am to suffer.
For you could by no means have
known what you suffer,
unless to you as Word
I had been sent by the Father.
You who saw what I *do*
saw (me) as suffering,
and when you saw, you did not stay,
but were wholly moved.
Being moved, go wisely to work,
you have me as a support,
rest in me.
Who I am, you shall know
when I go forth.
That for which they look on me now,
I am not;
what I am you shall see
when you come.
If you knew suffering,
you would have non-suffering.
Know suffering
and you will have non-suffering.
What you do not know
I myself will teach you.
I am your God,
not (the God) of the traitor.
I will to be in harmony

with holy souls to me.
Know the word of wisdom!
Say again to me,
"Glory be to you, Father!
Glory be to you, Word!
Glory be to you, holy Spirit!"'
'As for me,
if you would understand what I was:
Through the word I have made a jest of everything
and have not been made a jest at all.
I leaped;
but do you understand the whole,
and when you have understood it, say,
"Glory be to you, Father."' – 'Amen.'

Further Christ hymns from Nag Hammadi

The Gnostics were more productive in composing christological hymns than the church Christians. The various interpretations of the saving work of Christ were a fixed ingredient of Gnostic piety and poetry. Since not only poetic art but also, indeed particularly, christology was handed down in these hymns, the Christ hymns of the Gnostics met with rejection among the church Christians. In reaction, the Old Testament Psalter was established in worship as the only legitimate collection of hymns to Christ.[80] Thus in 210/212 Tertullian writes: 'For this purpose we also have the psalms, not those of the apostate, heretic and Platonist Valentinian, but the most holy and universally accepted psalms of the prophet David. He sings as of Christ; through him Christ himself has sung of himself' (*De carne* 20,3f.).

The following hymns come from the Nag Hammadi Library: as a rule they are in praise of Christ.[81] They differ in form; for the most part they are 'He is' predications. They are contained in different writings, but each could have come into being independently of these writings. They express central themes of Gnostic christology: the role of Christ as mediator between human beings and the transcendent Father, the apparent suffering of Christ (docetism), Christ as Word and Christ's humiliation as a work of salvation (cf. Phil. 2.7f.), Christ's honorific titles.

From the Tripartite Tractate

There is a hymnic acclamation in the Tripartite Tractate (see the Additional Material) which was probably originally an independent piece of tradition. This text expresses what has previously been discussed theoretically in the Tractate: only through the Son is the unknown Father knowable.

(NHC I 5; 66, 6ff.) Now he who arose from him when he stretched himself out for begetting and knowledge of the allnesses [...] he whom I name:

the form of the formless,
the body of the bodiless,
the face of the invisible,
the word of [the] inexplicable,
the mind of the inconceivable,
the fountain which flowed from him,
the root of those who are planted,
and the god of those who are laid down,
the light of those whom he enlightens,
the good pleasure of those in whom he has good pleasure,
the providence of those for whom he works providence,
the wisdom of those whom he has made wise,
the power of those to whom he gives power,
the assembly [of] those whom he assembles to himself,
the revelation of the things which are sought after,
the eye of those who see,
the breath of those who breathe,
the life of those who live,
the unity of those who are mixed with the allnesses.

From the Second Logos of the Great Seth

In the Second Logos of the Great Seth (NHC VII 2), a Gnostic revelation discourse of Christ to his followers, there is a hymn which describes the saving activity of Christ and his deception of the archons.

Its most prominent characteristic is a docetic christology: Christ did not really suffer and did not really die on the cross, but only apparently. This view was widespread among Gnostics who had repudiated everything corporeal (e.g. Apocalypse of Peter [NHC VII 3]; Irenaeus, *Haer.* I 24, 4 [on the Gnostic Basilides]).[82]

(NHC VII 2; 55,9ff.) And I was in the jaws of the lions.
And the plan which they devised about me (led) to the dissolving of their deception and their lack of understanding.
I did not give myself up to them as they had planned.
And I was not disturbed in any way, although they tormented me.
And I did not really die but only in semblance,
so that they would (not) put me to shame through them because these are a part of me.
I was removed from any shame,
and I was not anxious in the face of what had happened to me through them.
I was only apparently about to become a slave of fear,
but I suffered pain (only) in their sight and thought, so that a word will never be found to speak about them.
For my death which they think happened, (happened) to them only in their deception and their blindness, when they nailed their man to their death.
For their Ennoias did not see me.
For they were deaf and blind.
And in doing this, they condemn themselves.
Yes, they saw me; they tormented me.
(But) it was another, their father, who drank the gall and the vinegar; it was not I.
(Indeed) they struck me with the reed.
(But) it was another who bore the cross on his shoulders, Simon.[83]
It was another upon whose head they placed the crown of thorns.
But I was rejoicing in the height over all the (apparent) wealth of the archons and the seed of their deception, of their vain glory.
And I was laughing at their ignorance.

And I subjected all their powers.

For when I came down, no one saw me.

For I was altering my shapes, changing from one appearance to an(other) appearance.

And therefore, when I was at their gates, I assumed their likeness.

For I passed them by quietly, and I saw the places, and did not fear and was not ashamed, for I was undefiled.

And I was speaking with them, mingling with them through those who are mine and I trod on those who were strict on them in envy,

and I quenched the fire.

And I did all these things out of my will to accomplish what I willed by the will of the Father, who is above. (...)

From Melchizedek

In the Sethian writing Melchizedek (NHC IX 1), a revelation to Melchizedek, 'the king of Salem (...) the priest of God Most High' (Gen.14.18–20), only fragments of which have been preserved, there is a short hymn which possibly refers to Christ and can be read as a document of a docetic christology. Such paradoxical, apparently contradictory statements often occur in religious discourse (cf. above all Bronte [above, pp.60ff.]). The 'revelation of the mystery of the cross' in the Acts of John (97–102) has much in common with the hymn from Melchizedek. Cf. also the Christ hymn in the Acts of John 94–6.[84]

(NHC IX 1; 5,2ff.) He is unbegotten, though he has been begotten,

he does not eat, but truly he eats.

He does not drink, but truly he drinks.

He is uncircumcised, though he has been circumcised.

He is unfleshly, though he has come in the flesh.

He was not subject to suffering, *but* he had been subjected to suffering.

He did not rise from the dead, *though* he is risen from the dead.

From the Gospel of Truth

A hymn to the Word has been preserved in the Gospel of Truth (NHC I 3; cf. also the Additional Material). The Word is identified with Christ (cf. John 1). The notion that the Saviour is the word or the call occurs frequently in Gnostic texts (cf. simply the Trimorphic Protennoia). Salvation takes place in listening to the word (cf. here also the Gnostic awakening call).

(NHC I 3; 23,19ff.) While his wisdom is concerned with the Word,
and his teaching utters it,
his knowledge has revealed *it*.
While his honour is a crown upon it,
and his joy is bound up with it,
his glory has exalted it,
his form has revealed it,
his rest has received it into itself,
his love has made a body from it,
his faithfulness has embraced it.

In this way the Word of the Father goes forth into the All,
as the fruit [of] his heart and a manifestation of his will.
But it supports the All,
it chooses them
and receives back the manifestation of the All,
purifying them,
bringing them back into the father,
into the mother,
Jesus of the infinite sweetness.

From the Teachings of Silvanus

In many Gnostic revelation writings there are hymns which contain sayings about the Saviour. One example of this is the writing Teachings of Silvanus (NHC VII 4). It is one of the few not explicitly Gnostic documents within the Nag Hammadi writings; however, it was used by the Gnostics. The Teachings of Silvanus are wisdom teachings with a syncretistic stamp: Egyptian, biblical and Greek (above all Stoic) influences are tangible in them.

In the Teachings of Silvanus the frontiers between Gnosticism and the catholic church are still fluid. On the one hand they contain anti-Gnostic polemic (116, 5ff.); on the other the 'pneumatic' christology, the mention of the bridal chamber and the ascetic-dualistic statements show a close proximity to Gnosticism. This situation suggests a time of composition towards the end of the second century in Alexandria.

The first Christ hymn from the 'Teachings of Silvanus' quoted here is strongly reminiscent of the hymn contained in Paul's letter to the Philippians.[85] In form it is a depiction of the acts of Christ. Such summaries were very popular in apocryphal Christian literature (e.g. Pistis Sophia 110; Acts of Thomas 47) and have their starting point in the New Testament (e.g. Luke 7.21ff.). They are also abundantly attested in the Nag Hammadi writings.[86] The descent of Christ into the underworld (= world) is often associated with the depiction of his acts. His descent brings about the conquest of the archons and the salvation of humankind.[87] This motif (cf. also Eph. 4.7–10; I Peter 3.19f.) became very widespread in early Christian piety and often took on romance-like features (cf. e.g. the Gospel of Bartholomew). However, the descent into the underworld is not tied to the person of Jesus; among other things the motif also appears with other Gnostic saviour figures as e.g. in the Trimorphic Protennoia (NHC XIII 1) and the Paraphrase of Shem (NHC VII 1), and also in the Pronoia hymn from the Apocryphon of John (NHC II 1; 30,11ff.).[88]

By contrast, the second hymn from the Teachings of Silvanus mainly consists of a collection of designations of Christ of the kind that often occur in Christian literature (cf. e.g. the Christ hymn from the Tripartite Tractate, p.71, or the eucharistic prayer from the Acts of John, pp.107f.).

(NHC VII 4; 110,14ff.) Know who Christ is,
and make him your friend,
for this is the friend who is trustworthy.
He is also the God and the Teacher.
This one, although he was God, became human for your sake.
It is this one who shattered the iron bars of the underworld[89]
and the bronze bolts.
It is this one who attacked and cast down every haughty tyrant.

It is he who loosened from himself the fetters with which he was
bound.
He brought up the poor from the depth and the troubled from
the underworld.
It is he who humbled the haughty powers;
he who put to shame arrogance through humility;
he who has cast down the strong and the boaster through
weakness;
he who in his shame scorned that which is considered an
honour, so that the humble for God's sake might be highly
exalted;
(and) he who has put on humanity, yet is God, the divine Word,
he who bears humanity[90] at all times.
And he willed to produce humility in the arrogant.
He who has exalted humankind came to resemble God,
not in order that he might bring God down to humankind, but
that humankind might become like God.

O this great goodness of God!
O Christ, king, you who have revealed to humankind the great
divinity, king of every virtue and king of life,
king of the aeons and greatest of the heavens,
hear my words and forgive me!

(NHC VII 4; 112,33ff.) He (it is) who has come forth from your
mouth and in your heart,
the firstborn,
the wisdom,
the prototype,
the first light.
For he is light from the power of God,
and he is an emanation of the pure glory of the Almighty.
And he is the spotless mirror of the working of God,
and he is the image of his goodness.
For he is also the light of the eternal light.
He is the seeing which looks at the invisible Father,
he always serves and forms by the Father's will.
He alone was begotten by the good pleasure of the Father.

For he is an incomprehensible word,
and he is wisdom and life.
He animates and nourishes all living beings and powers.
Just as a soul gives life to all the members (of the body),
(so) he rules over all with power and gives them life.
For he is the beginning and the end of everyone,
he looks on all and encompasses all.
He is concerned for everyone, and he rejoices, and he is also again troubled.
On the one hand, he is troubled for those who have inherited the place of punishment as their lot; on the other hand, he is concerned for all those whom he brings to instruction only with great toil.
But he rejoices over everyone who is in purity.

From the Interpretation of Knowledge

The Interpretation of Knowledge (NHC XI 1) is unfortunately preserved only in very fragmentary form. The legible text shows clear Gnostic (Valentinian) influences;[91] it can be divided into two parts: 1. Christ as head saves his body, the church (pages 9–15) ; 2. the second part contains an account of the way in which the members of the church are to behave towards one another (pages 15–21). Here the ecclesiological notions from I Corinthians and Ephesians/Colossians are determinative.[92] In form the text represents a homily and shows characteristics of the diatribe style.

The following 'I am' hymn stands out from the context in that as a quotation of Christ the Teacher it is clearly distinct from the admonition of the author of the homily.[93] The hymn represents a promise of salvation to the soul and thus can be included among the numerous Gnostic writings about the soul. As in the case of the first hymn from the Teachings of Silvanus (cf. above, pp.75f.), reference is made back to the Philippians hymn:

(NHC XI 1; 10,27ff.): Likewise I have become very small,
so that through my humiliation I might take you up to the great height,
the place whence you had fallen.
You were brought to this pit.

If now you believe in me,
it is I who shall take you above through this shape that you see.
It is I who shall bear you upon my shoulders.
Enter through the rib,[94]
the place whence you came.

And hide yourself from the wild beasts.
The burden[95] that you bear, now it [is] not yours (...).
When you go [...].

The awakening call

Salvation takes place through the knowledge of forgotten truth. The Gnostic imagines this disastrous forgetting as sleep or drunkenness. The Gnostic Saviour figure has the task of arousing the sleeping soul and opening its eyes to its true origin. This event of salvation is set in motion by the awakening call. Thus there are formulations of the awakening call in many Gnostic revelation writings.[96]

From the Trimorphic Protennoia

The Trimorphic Protennoia (NHC XIII 1) is a revelation discourse of a female Gnostic saviour. In form it displays similarities to Bronte ('I Am' sayings, see above, pp.6off.). The notion of the divine revealer as a call is a central one in this writing:

Thus the Trimorphic Protennoia represents a self-revelation of the personified 'first thought of the primal Father'. This self-revelation is divided into three discourses, in each of which the function of the awakening call and its designation are different (discourse of the Protennoia = call; discourse of Heimarmene = voice; discourse of the Logos = word).

(NHC XIII 1; 36,9ff.) Through me knowledge comes forth.
[I] dwell in the ineffable and unknowable (viz. aeons).
I am perception and knowledge,
uttering a voice by means of a thought.
[I] am the existing voice; I cry out in everyone,
and they know it (viz. the cry), because a seed is in [them](...).

From the Second Apocalypse of James

The Second Apocalypse of James is a revelation discourse of James which hands on a summons to knowledge and to knowing the Saviour, which amounts to an awakening call.

(NHC V 4; 59,12ff.) But you have judged [yourselves], and because of this you will remain in your fetters.
You have burdened yourselves, and you will repent, (but) you will have no profit at all.
Behold him who speaks and seek him who is silent.
Know him who has come to this place, and understand him who has left (it).

From the Concept of Our Great Power

The notion of the awakening call also occurs in this Gnostic tractate.

(NHC VI 4; 39,33ff.) You still sleep and dream dreams. Wake up and return, taste and eat the true food! Distribute the word and the water of life! Cease from the evil lusts and desires and (the teachings of the) Anomoeans[97] – evil heresies that do not endure.

From Corpus Hermeticum VII

The notion of the awakening call is widespread in the Hermetica.

(CH VII 1f.) Where are you going, people, drunkards who have drunk yourself stupid with the unmixed word of ignorance? (...) Stop and become sober, look up with the eyes of the heart! (...) Seek a guide on the way who will guide you to the doors of knowledge, where is the radiant light which is free of darkness, where no one is drunk but all are sober and look with the heart on the one who wills to be seen!

From Poimandres

In the Hermetic tractate Poimandres (see above, p.34) the recipient of revelation wants to summon men and women to knowledge.

(CH I 27f.) You people, you men and women of the earth! You who have given yourselves over to drunkenness and sleep, to ignorance of God! Become sober! Cease to be drunk, bewitched by unreasoning sleep (...)! Why have you surrendered yourselves to death, you men and women of the earth? For you have the right to share in immortality. Repent! You who have followed the way of error! You who make common cause with ignorance! Depart from the dark light! Take your share of immortality! Forsake corruption!

From the Apocryphon of John

At the end of his revelation discourse (see above, pp.19f.), the Gnostic Saviour, who in the Apocryphon of John is identified with Christ, utters the following awakening call:

(NHC II 1; 31,14ff.) Arise and remember! For you are those who have heard (my call). Follow your root, which is I, the compassionate one! And guard yourself against the angels of poverty and the demons of chaos and all those who ensnare you! And beware of the deep sleep and the enclosure of the inside of the underworld!

From the Teachings of Silvanus

There are also sections in the wisdom writing 'The Teachings of Silvanus' (see above, pp.74ff.) which resemble an awakening call.

(NHC VII 4; 88,24ff.) [...] End the sleep which weighs heavily upon you! Depart from the forgetfulness which fills you with darkness! (NHC VII 4; 92,10ff.) But before all other words, know your birth. Know yourself, from what substance you are, and from what race you are and from what species! (NHC VII 4; 94,19ff.) O soul, (you) stubborn (soul), be sober and shake off your drunkenness, which is the work of ignorance. If you persist (thus) and live in the body, you exist in roughness. When you entered into bodily birth, you were brought forth. (Now) you have come inside the bridal chamber and you are illuminated in mind. (NHC VII 4; 102,34ff.) My child, do not allow your mind to stare downwards, but rather let it look upwards at things in the light. For the light always comes from above. Even if it (viz. your mind) is upon the earth, let it seek to pursue the things above. Enlighten your mind with the light of heaven so that you turn to the light of heaven.

From the Odes of Solomon

There is also an awakening call from the saviour figure in the Odes of Solomon:

(OdSol 33,6ff.) You sons of men, repent
and you, their daughters, come hither!
And leave the ways of this corruption and approach me!
And I will enter into you!
And I will lead you out of annihilation!
And I will bestow wisdom upon you in the ways of truth!
You shall not fall victim to corruption, nor to annihilation!
Hearken to me and be saved.
For I proclaim[98] the grace of God among you!
And through me you are to be saved and are to be blessed.
Your judge, it is I!
And those who have put me on will not fall into disgrace.
Rather, they will possess incorruption in the new world.
My elect, walk in me!
And I will teach my ways to those who seek me!
And promise them my name!
Hallelujah![99]

From Zostrianos

In Zostrianos (NHC VIII 1) the divinized Zostrianos preaches to the ignorant after his heavenly journey. This preaching displays the typical features of the awakening call: the demand for repentance and knowledge, the turning away from error and matter.

(NHC VIII 1; 130,16ff.) Understand, you who live, the holy seed of Seth. Do not be inattentive to me. [Awaken] your divine part to God, and strengthen the sinless, elect soul. And look on the dissolution of this world and seek the immutable un-bornness. The [Father] of all these things invites you, although (others) reject you.

And although others treat you unjustly, he will not abandon you. Do not baptize yourselves with death, nor entrust yourselves to those who are inferior to you instead of to those who are elect.

Flee from the madness and the fetters of femaleness and choose for yourselves the deliverance of maleness. You have not come to suffer, but you have come to escape your fetters. Free yourselves, and that which has bound you will be dissolved.

Save yourselves, so that that one there (viz. your soul) may be saved. The kind Father has sent you the Saviour and given you strength. Why do you hesitate? Seek when you are sought. When you are invited, listen. For the time is short. Do not be led astray. Great is the aeon of the aeons of the living ones, (but also) the [chastisement] of those who have not attained to agreement. Many fetters and chastizers surround you.
Flee quickly, before death reaches you. Look at the light.
Avoid the darkness. Do not be led astray to your destruction.

The sacrament of dying [Apolytrosis]

The 'sacrament of dying' is practised in Gnosticism so that the soul of the Gnostic is equipped for its ascent after death (cf. the Mandaean ceremony of the ascent of the soul). Before the soul can unite with the Pleroma, however, it has to make its way past the archons. These want to seize hold of it, so the soul must become 'invisible' and/or be able to give the correct answers to the questions of the archons (passwords). This topic is central in the Books of Jeu and there are also echoes of it in the Naassene Psalm.

The Gnostic sacrament of dying has led to specific liturgical forms. The 'Gnostic catechisms', for example, which inculcate the correct answers to the questions of the archons, are to be put in the context of this sacrament as it has been handed down by Irenaeus, *Haer*. I 21, 5 (see below, pp.146f.). The witnessing formulae which are to be found for example in the Paraphrase of Shem or in Origen's account of the Ophites also have their origin in the sacrament of dying. Only through the correct testimony can the soul complete its ascent.

From the Apocalypse of Paul

The Apocalypse of Paul describes a heavenly journey by the apostle Paul in which Paul gets to the tenth heaven. In the seventh heaven he meets an old man who could represent the creator God.[100]

(NHC V 2; 23,1ff.) The old man spoke, saying [to me], 'Where are you going, Paul, O blessed one and the one who was set apart from his mother's womb?'[101] And I looked at the Spirit, and he was nodding his head, saying to me, 'Speak with him!' And I replied, saying to the old man, 'I want to go to the place from which I came.' And the old man replied to me, 'Where have you come from?' And I replied and said, 'I am going down to the world of the dead in order to lead captive the captivity[102] that was led captive in the captivity of Babylon.'[103] The old man replied to me and said, 'How will you be able to get away from me? Look and see these authorities and these powers.' [The] Spirit spoke, saying, 'Give him [the] sign that you have, and [he will] open for you.'

From the First Apocalypse of James

The First Apocalypse of James is a revelation dialogue between Jesus and James in which Jesus gives James the following advice.

(NHC V 3; 33,11ff.): When you come into their power, one of them who is their supervisor will say to you, 'Who are you or where do you come from?' You are to say to him, 'I am a son, and I come from the Father.' He will say to you, 'What sort of son are you, and to what father do you belong?' You are to say to him, 'I come from the Pre-[existent] Father, and I am a son of the Pre-existent One.' (...) When he also says to you, 'Where do you want to go?', you are to say to him, 'To the place from which I have come, there shall I return.' And if you say these things, you will escape their attacks.[104]

From the Gospel of Thomas

There is also a 'Gnostic catechism' in the Gospel of Thomas, a collection of sayings of Jesus, some of which have a Gnostic stamp.

(NHC II 2; 41,31ff.) Jesus said, 'If they say to you, "Where did you come from?", say to them, "We come from the light, the place where the light came into being of its own accord and established [itself] and became manifest through their image." If they say to you, "Who are you?," then say, "We are its sons, and we are the elect of the living father." If they ask you, "What is the sign of your father in you?," say to them, "It is movement and repose."'

From the Gospel of Philip in Epiphanius

The church father Epiphanius quotes from a Gospel of Philip.[105] This quotation is an 'aid to ascent' for the soul of the Gnostic.

(Epiphanius, *Haer.* 26, 13, 2) The Lord revealed to me what the soul must say as she ascends into heaven, and how she (must) answer each of the higher powers, as follows: 'I have known myself,' she says, 'and I gathered myself from every side; I have sowed no children for the archon, but I have uprooted his roots and I gathered the members that were scattered. And I know who you are. For I,' she says, 'belong to those from on high.' And so she thinks that she will be set free.

From the Paraphrase of Shem

The Paraphrase of Shem is a revelation writing from Nag Hammadi in which the recipient of the revelation is carried away in ecstasy and is instructed by the revelation discourses from heavenly persons. It also contains a testimony of Shem to his ascent.

(NHC VII 1; 45,34ff.). My time was completed. And my mind put on the immortal memory. And I said, 'I agree with your memory which you have revealed to me, Elorchaie, and you, Amoiaia, and you, Sederkea, and your guilelessness, Strophea, and you, Chelkeak, and you, Chelkea, and Chelke and Elaie. You are the immortal memory. I testify by you, spark, (you who are) the unquenchable one, you who are an eye of heaven and a voice of light, and (I testify by) Sophaia and Saphaia and Saphaina and the righteous spark and faith, the first and the last, and the upper and the lower air, and by you, Chelkeak and Chelke and Elaios. You are the immortal memory.

I testify by you, spark, (you who are) the unquenchable one, who are an eye of heaven and a voice of light, and Sophaia, and Saphaia, and Saphaina, and the righteous spark, and faith, the first and the last, and the upper and the lower air and to all the powers and forces that are in the creation. And by you, impure light, and by you also, east and west, south and north. You are the zones of the inhabited world.

And (I bear witness) also by you, Molychtha and Essoch, you who are the root of evil and every work and (every) impure effort of nature. These are the (things) which I have completed, and I bear witness. I am Shem.[106]

Ophite formulae of ascent

The Alexandrian theologian Origen, writing in the third century CE, reports on the formulae of ascent which are used by the Ophites, a Gnostic group in which the serpent cult played a major role.

(Origen, *Contra Celsum* VI 31)(...) (When they [viz., the Ophites] have gone through their so-called 'Barrier of Evil', they say): '*I greet the gates of the archons, bound for eternity, the solitary king, the fetter of blindness, uncaring oblivion, the first power, which is preserved by the spirit of providence and by wisdom, from where I will be sent in total purity, being already part of the light of the Son and of the Father. May grace be with me, yes Father, may it be with me.*' Here, according to their information, the Ogdoad begins.

Then they are taught to say these words as they pass through the one they call Ialdabaoth: '*And you, Ialdabaoth, first and seventh, born to command with confidence, ruling word of the pure mind, perfect work for Son and Father, I bring the symbol of life in the form of a picture; I have opened to the world the gate which you had closed for your time, and pass by your power free again. May grace be with me, Father, may it be with me.*' They assert that this ruler with the face of a lion is related to the star Phainon (= Saturn).

Then they think that the person who has passed through Ialdabaoth and reached Iao (= Jupiter) must say: '*And you, Iao, ruler of the hidden mysteries of the Son and Father, you who shine by night, you second and first, lord of death, portion of the guiltless, in now bringing you my own submissive disposition as a symbol, I am ready to pass by your kingdom. You have empowered the one who has come into being through you with living words. May grace be with me, Father, may it be with me.*'

Then (they mention) Sabaoth (= Mars), whom they think one should address thus: '*Ruler of the fifth kingdom, prince Sabaoth, defender of the law of your creation which is liberated by grace, by a more potent pentad (= fifth), see the blameless symbol of your art, and let me pass by, preserved by the image of a picture, a body set free by the pentad. May grace be with me, Father, may it be with me.*'

Then[107] they mention Astaphaeus (= Venus), whom they believe one should address thus: '*Astaphaeus, ruler of the third gate, guardian of the primal spring of water, look on me as an initiate, who has been cleansed by the spirit of the virgin, and let me pass, you who see the substance of the world essence. May grace be with me, Father, may it be with me.*'

And after him (they mention) Ailoaeus, to whom they think

one must speak these words: '*Ailoaeus, ruler of the second gate, let me pass. I bring to you a symbol of your mother, grace, which is hidden in the forces of the powers. May grace be with me, Father, may it be with me.*'

Finally they mention Horaeus (= the moon), and think one should say to him: '*You who have fearlessly passed beyond the wall of fire and have received the rule over the first gate, Horaeus, let me pass. For you see the symbol of your power cast down by a picture of the tree of life, an image taken in the likeness of an innocent man. May grace be with me, Father, may it be with me.*'[108]

Gnostic prayers on dying

In the Second Apocalypse of James and in the Acts of Thomas, prayers have been handed down which are spoken by the apostles James or Thomas before their execution. These two prayers before dying show parallels to some Manichaean Jesus psalms and Pistis Sophia psalms. In all these prayers the petition for a smooth ascent of the soul after death stands in the foreground. Perhaps these prayers are to be put in the liturgical context of the sacrament of dying.[109]

Prayer of James before his execution

(NHC V 4; 62,16ff.) My God and my Father,
(you) who saved me from this dead hope,
(you) who made me alive through a mystery of your will.
Do not let the days of this world become too long for me,
but the day of your [light ...]!
Redeem me from this [place of] sojourn!
Do not let your grace depart from me,
but may your grace become pure!
Save me from an evil death!
Bring me alive from the grave,
because your grace is alive in me,
the longing to collaborate in the work of fulfilment!

Deliver me from the sinful flesh,
for I have trusted in you with all my strength!
For you are the life of life,
deliver me from a humiliating enemy!
Do not give me into the hand of a judge
who is strict with sin!
Forgive me all the guilt of (my) days!
For I live in you,
your grace lives in me.
I have denied everyone,
but you I have openly confessed.
Deliver me from evil affliction!
But now is the [time] and the hour.
O Holy [Spirit], send [me] salvation!
Light [from] light (...).

Prayer of Thomas before his execution

(Acts of Thomas 167): O my Lord and my God,
and (my) hope and (my) redeemer,
and (my) leader and (my) guide in all the lands!
Be with all who serve you,
and lead me today, who come to you today.
Let no one take my soul
which I have committed to you.
Do not let the toll collectors see me
and do not let the exactors of tribute accuse me falsely!
The serpent is not to see me,
and the dragon's brood is not to hiss on me!
Behold, Lord, I have fulfilled your work
and accomplished your command.
I have become a slave;
therefore today l am receiving freedom. Give it now and fulfil
it!
(...)

A (Sethian) ritual of ascent

The Three Steles of Seth (NHC VII 5) belong among the Nag Hammadi writings which are attributed to Sethian Gnosis.[110] The writing displays no Christian influences; rather, it is associated with Middle or Neoplatonic and Jewish[111] thought. The threefold recitation of particular lines (e.g. 120,34ff. etc.) indicates liturgical usage.

The *Sitz im Leben* of the Three Steles of Seth is the liturgy. From the statements in the last section we may conclude that the Three Steles of Seth is evidence of a Sethian mystery of ascent. Here reference should be made to the Gnostic apocalypses Zostrianos (NHC VIII 1) and Allogenes (NHC XI 3), and with qualifications also to Marsanes (NHC X 1) and the ritual of ascent in the Trimorphic Protennoia (see the Additional Material, p.141). Almost all these texts are reports of the heavenly journeys of the recipients of revelation in the first person and stamped by their ascent to ever higher knowledge. Perfecting takes place through instruction by mythological entities and sacraments (baptisms [see here the baptisms of Zostrianos, below, pp.94f.], anointings, crownings). All these ascent accounts have close parallels with one another and with the Three Steles of Seth in terminology, mythology and content, so that we can assume that they reflect the religious feelings of a particular Gnostic group, the so-called Sethian Gnostics.[112] It is thought that these Gnostics knew two sacraments, baptism and the mystery of ascent. The Three Steles of Seth could have represented the liturgical text for this Sethian sacrament, whereas the heavenly journeys mentioned above could have been a kind of edifying religious literature in the context of this sacrament.

In terms of content, the Three Steles of Seth consist of three hymns which are devoted to the Autogenes, the Barbelo and the Unbegotten Father.

(NHC VII 5; 118,10ff.) The revelation of Dositheos about the three steles of Seth,[113] the father of the living and immovable race, which (the steles) he (viz. Dositheos) saw and understood. And after he had read them (the steles), he remembered them. And he gave them to the elect, as they were inscribed there.

Many times I have[114] joined in offering praise with the powers. And I have been made worthy by the immeasurable magnitudes.

Now they (viz. the steles) are as follows:

The first stele of Seth:
I praise you, Father, Gerdama,
I, as your (own) son, Emmacha Seth,
whom you brought forth without birth,
as a blessing of our God.
For I am your (own) son.
And you are my mind, my father.
And I, I have sowed, and I begot;
[but] you, you have [seen] the magnitudes.
You have stood
imperishable.
I praise you, Father.
Bless me, Father.[115]
For it is because of you that I exist.
It is because of God that you exist.
For because of you I exist with that one (viz. God).
You are light,
for you have seen light.
You have revealed light.
You are Mirotheas.
You are my Mirotheos.
I praise you as God.
I praise your divinity.
(...)
You have saved,
you have saved,
you have saved us,
crown-bearer, crown-bestower.
We praise you for ever.
We praise you,
(we) who have been saved,
(we) as the perfect individuals;
we are perfect on account of you,
those who [have been made] perfect with you.
(...)
You are perfect,
you are perfect,

you are perfect.
The first stele of Seth

The second stele of Seth:
Great is the first aeon,
(the) male virgin Barbelo,
the first glory of the invisible Father,
she who is called 'perfect'.
(...)
You are an elect monad (= unity),
the first [shadow] of the holy Father,
light from light.
[We] praise you,
(you who are) producer of perfection,
aeon-giver.
(...)
Because for their sake you have empowered the eternal ones
through being.
You have empowered divinity through living.
You have empowered knowledge through goodness.
Through blessedness you have empowered the shadows
which pour from the one.
You have empowered the one through knowledge.
You have empowered another one through creation.
You have empowered him who is of equal birth
and him who is not equal,
him who is similar
and him who is not similar.
(...)
Through you salvation has come to us.
From you is salvation.
You are wisdom;
you are knowledge;
you are truth;
through you is life;
from you is life.
Through you is mind;
from you is mind.

You are a mind,
you are a world;
you are the truth;
you are a triple power;
you are threefold.
Truly you are thrice,
the aeon of aeons.
(...)
Unite us,
as you have been united.
Teach us [these] things
which you see.
Give [us] power,
that we may be saved to eternal life.
(...)
You have heard!
You have heard!
You have saved!
You have saved!
We give thanks!
We praise you always!
We shall glorify you!
The second stele of Seth

The third stele:
We rejoice!
We rejoice!
We rejoice!
We have seen!
We have seen!
We have seen
the one who truly first exists,
that he truly exists,
that he is the first eternal one.
(You) unborn, from you are the eternal ones and the aeons,
the all-perfect ones who are in a place
and the perfect individuals.
We praise you,

you who are without being,
the existence which is before (other) existences,
the first being which is before (other) beings,
the Father of divinity and life,
the creator of the mind,
the giver of the good,
the giver of blessedness.
We all praise you, knowing one.
(....)
You are one,
you are a single living spirit.
How shall we give (you) a name?
We do not have it;
for you are the existence of them all.
You are the life of them all.
You are the mind of them all.
(...)
We praise you,
for we have been saved.
Always we praise you.
For this reason we shall praise you,
so that we may be saved to an eternal salvation.
We have praised you,
because we are able.
We have been saved,
because you have always wished
us to do all this.
(...)

The one who will remember these (words) and praise at all time
is to become perfect among those who are perfect and without
pain in any respect. For they all praise these (viz. Autogenes,
Barbelo, Unbegotten Father), individually and together. And
afterwards they shall be silent. And thus, as it has been determined for them, they ascend.

After the silence, they descend from the third. They praise the
second, after (both) these the first. The way of ascent is the way
of descent.

Know now, as those who live, that you have attained (viz. knowledge). And you taught yourselves the infinite things. Marvel at the truth which is within them, and the revelation.

The Three Steles of Seth. This book belongs to the fatherhood. It is the son who wrote it. Bless me, O father. I praise you, father, in peace. Amen.[116]

Baptisms and anointings

The Gnostics also had baptisms, washings and anointings (see also in the Additional Material, pp.141ff.). These functioned less as rites of purification than as means of achieving different degrees of knowledge and thus prepared the way into new and higher stages of being.

From Zostrianos

As an example of a Gnostic baptismal text here is a section from Zostrianos (NHC VIII 1). The content of this writing is a heavenly journey by Zostrianos. As with Shem in the Paraphrase of Shem (NHC VII 1), the (ecstatic) separation from the body is a presupposition for the heavenly journey. On this journey Zostrianos is given saving knowledge through visions and revelation dialogues with mythological figures. The cultural background to these visions in Zostrianos is, first, influenced by Neoplatonic thought material; secondly, the thought is close to Sethian Gnosticism. There are many 'short forms' in Zostrianos like prayers, paraeneses, liturgical vowel series etc. These liturgical forms also include the following baptismal liturgy which reports no less than five baptisms of Zostrianos (with the aim of deification; for a similar ceremony see p.141 and the Three Steles of Seth).[117]

(NHC VIII 1; 6,7ff.) And I was baptized in the [name of] the divine Autogenes [by] those powers which are [upon] (the) living waters, Michar and Mi[cheus]. And I was purified by [the] great Barpharanges.[118] And they [revealed] themselves to me (and) wrote me in glory.[119] I was sealed by those who are over these powers, [Michar], Mi[ch]eus, Seldao, Ele[nos], and Zogenethlos. And I [became] a [root]-seeing angel. And I stood upon the first aeon – that is the fourth – together with the souls. I praised the divine Autogenes and the forefather Geradama, [...] the Autogenes, the first perfect [human], and Seth Emm[acha Seth], the son of [A]damas, the [father of] the [immovable race] and the [four] [lights...] [...] and Mirothea, the mother [...] [...] and Prophania [...] of the lights and De[...] [...].

And I was [baptized for the] second time in the name of the divine Autogenes by the same powers. I became an angel of the male race. And I stood upon the second aeon – that is the third – together with the children of Seth. I praised each of them.

And I was baptized for the third time in the name of the divine Autogenes by each of these powers. [I] became a holy angel. And I stood upon the third [aeon] – that is the second. I [praised] each of them.

And I was baptized for the fourth time by [each of] these powers. I became [a] perfect [angel]. [And I stood upon] the fourth aeon – [that is the first] – and [I praised each of them] [...].[120]

[When I was] baptized for the fifth [time] in the name of the Autogenes by each of these powers, I became divine. (And) [I] stood upon the fifth aeon – which is a prior stage [of them (viz. aeons)] all. I saw all those who belong to [the] Autogenes, (namely) those who really exist.

And I was baptized five times.

From the Gospel of the Egyptians

The Gospel of the Egyptians[121] from Nag Hammadi hands down a prayer which is embedded in a baptismal context (NHC III 2; 66,1–8). Strictly speaking, the baptismal hymn can be divided into two parts. It is impossible to discover precisely who is addressed in the first part, which consists of five short strophes with the same structure: probably it is Jesus or Jesseus Mazareus Jessedekeus, a mythological figure of Sethian Gnosticism who carries out holy baptisms.[122] The second part differs: it is addressed to a divine triad or quaternity (God the Father, the Mother, Jesus the Son and a further light-being). The marked use of magical vowels indicates a fluid transition between religion and magic.[123]

(NHC III 2; 66,8ff.) iē ieus ēō ou ēō ōūa!
Really truly,
Jesseus Mazareus Jessedekeus,
living water,
child of the child,
glorious name.

Really truly,
being aeon,
iii ēēēē eeee oooo uuuu ōōōō aaa!

Really truly,
ēi aaaa ōōōō, (you) who are,
(you) who see the aeons!

Really truly,
aee ēēē iii uuuuu ōōōōōōōō,
(you) who are to all eternity.

Really truly,
iēa aiō in the heart,
(you) who are,
son for ever to eternity,
you are what you are,
you are who you are.[124]

This great name of yours is upon me,
(you) self-begotten perfect one,
(you) who are not outside me.
I see you, you who are invisible to everyone.
For who will be able to comprehend you with another voice?
Because I have known you, I have (now) mixed with the immutable.
I have armed myself with an armour of light.

I have become light.
For the Mother was at that place because of the fair splendour
of grace.
Therefore I stretched out my folded hands.
I received form in the circle of the riches of the light
which is in my bosom, which gives form to many begotten ones
through the light,
which no complaint reaches.
I shall proclaim your glory truly,
for I have comprehended you,
sou iēs ide aeiō aeie ois,
O aeon, aeon,
God of silence.
I honour you completely.
You are my resting place,
(you) son,
ēsēso e,
(you) formless one
who exist in the formless ones,
who exist, to awaken the human being,
through whom you will to purify me
into your life, according to your imperishable name.
Therefore the incense of life is in me.
I have mixed it with water after the model of all archons,
in order that I may live with you in the peace of the saints,
you who exist really truly for ever.

Baptism and anointing among the Valentinians

Documents of Valentinian sacramental piety have been preserved in
Nag Hammadi Codex XI. However, the pages of the codex are in a
very bad state. Consequently these prayers will not be reproduced
complete, and only extracts from the sections which can best be
reconstructed will be cited here.

(NHC XI 2; 40,11ff.) (...) It is fitting for [you now] to send your
son [Jesus] Christ and to anoint us so that we may be able to

trample [upon] the [snakes] and [the heads] of the scorpions[125] and [the whole] power of the devil, since he is the shepherd [of the seed].

Through him (viz. Christ) we [have] known you. And we [glorify] you: '[Glory] be to you, the Father in the [Son, the Father] in the Son, the Father [in the] holy [church and in the] holy [angels]! From now on he abides [for ever in] the perpetuity of the aeons, for ever until the [untraceable] aeons of the aeons. Amen.

(NHC XI 2; 42,10ff.) [... from the] world [into the Jordan] and from [the blindness] of the world [into the sight of] God, from [the carnal] into the spiritual, [from] the physical [into the] angelic, from [the created] into the Pleroma, [from] the world [into the aeon], from the [servitudes] into (the) sonship, [from] divisions [into community], from [the desert into] our village, from [the cold into] the hot [...].[126]

Hymn for the anointing from the Acts of Thomas

In the Acts of Thomas, which contains further documents of Gnostic spirituality, there is also an anointing prayer.

(Acts of Thomas 27) Come, holy name of Christ that is exalted above every name!
Come, power of the Most High and perfect compassion!
Come, highest gift of grace!
Come, compassionate mother!
Come, fellowship with the male!
Come, revealer of the hidden mysteries;
Come, Mother of the seven houses, that you may be given rest in the eighth house.
Come, +messenger+ of the five members: mind,

thought, insight, consideration, reason.
Have fellowship with these young people!
Come, Holy Spirit, and purify their reins and their heart.
And give them the added seal in the name of (the) Father and
(the) Son and (the) Holy Spirit!

The bridal chamber

The bridal chamber has its background in the notion of hermaphro-
ditic unity. Perfection consists in the unity of male and female pairs. If
this unity is destroyed, perfection comes to an end. This becomes clear
from the Sophia myth: when Sophia wanted to bring forth something
without her male pair, her creation became defective and the world
arose. Salvation takes place through the abolition of this separation;
just as Sophia again turns to her pair, so too must the human soul by
returning to its origin. This salvation is realized through the sacrament
of the bridal chamber. The most important genuinely Gnostic evidence
about the sacrament of the bridal chamber, which was already known
to the church fathers and often fell victim to their polemic, is probably
the Exegesis of the Soul and the Gospel of Philip (see Additional
Material) from Nag Hammadi. But further poetic texts, too, attest this
typically Gnostic sacrament.

The Mandaean rite of investiture

The following evidence from specifically Mandaean religion belongs to
the rite of investiture. Along with the rites of anointing and crowning,
this stands between baptism and the bridal chamber *(kushta)*. Simul-
taneously with the mythical investiture of the Manda dHaije,[127] the
'bridegroom', the Mandaean initiate, is invested and thus is prepared
for the bridal chamber. The Mandaean initiate also wears the garments
and the crown which are bestowed on him in this sacrament at his
burial and the sacrament of dying. Through the sacramental action the
initiate is taken up into the person of the Saviour Manda dHaije.

(ML 237) In the name of the great life.
On the day when they created the breeches Nsab[128] for the

Manda dHaije,
his splendour arose over the eggs.[129]
Over the eggs his splendour arose.
When the women looked on the splendour of the Manda
dHaije, they said to one another:
'Whence comes this splendour which has arisen over us?'
Thereupon the young man who stood before them replied:
'This splendour comes from the breeches Nsab of the Manda
dHaije.'
All the women stand on the roofs,
bless Manda dHaije and say to him:
'May you be blessed, our father Manda dHaije,
and blessed be he who has made you these garments,
whose splendour is so rich.'
(Give him some drink.)[130]

Inscriptions on the bridal chamber

In the following epitaph of the Gnostic woman Flavia Sophe the significance of the bridal chamber as a means of immortality becomes clear.
The inscription presumably comes from the second century CE. The
sacraments like anointing, the central role of the bridal chamber and
the terror of the earthly spheres of archons on the ascent of the soul
point to its Valentinian character.

A further Gnostic inscription from the second century was found in
the Via Latina alongside the epitaph of the Gnostic woman Flavia
Sophe. This inscription, too, clearly has Valentinian features and particularly in respect of the idea of the bridal chamber shows very close
similarities to the Gospel of Philip (NHC II 3; cf. sayings 82; 87; 102;
122; 124; 127).

Both inscriptions are composed in metric form and indicate a high
degree of education on the part of the authors. That they were found
on the Via Latina shows that there were Valentinians among the
Christians of Rome.[131]

Epitaph of the Gnostic woman Sophe

You who long for the fatherly light,
sister, spouse, my Sophe,
anointed in the baths of Christ with imperishable, cleansing,
anointing oil,
you have hastened to look on the divine countenances of the
aeons,
the great angel of the great counsel (viz. the Saviour),
the true son;
you came into the bridal chamber and [immortal] you arose
[into the bosom of] the Father.

This dead woman did not have an ordinary turning point in life.
She died and lives and sees a truly imperishable light.
She lives to the living and truly died to the dead.
O earth, how do you wonder at the nature of (her) mortal shell?
Are you terrified?

Inscription on the bridal chamber

My [brothers] of the bridal chambers who lay me [to rest] light
me with torches,
they deeply long for feasts[132] in our [dwellings],
lauding the Father and praising the Son,
from where is the outflow from the one [silence] and the truth.

A bridal hymn

The following bridal hymn comes from the Acts of Thomas.[133] It is
modelled on Syrian wedding songs (the bride and bridegroom as a
royal couple, the throne as an overturned sled, etc.). However, this is
not a profane wedding song, but is a testimony to Gnostic religious
feeling. This is suggested by formulations like 'daughter of light', etc.
The bride symbolizes Sophia: like the soul in the Exegesis of the Soul
(see Additional Material), she is decorated and waits for her pair and
saviour.

The hymn also promises the wedding feast of the bridal couple with all who are liberated. Here there seems to be an allusion to the future consummation, which takes place when all the sparks of light have returned to their origin (cf. Irenaeus, *Haer.* I 30, 14).

(Acts of Thomas 6f.) The maiden is the daughter of light.
Upon her stands and rests the majestic splendour of kings,
proud and delightful is her gaze,
she is radiant with shining beauty.
Her garments are like spring flowers,
a scent of sweet fragrance is diffused from them.
On her head dwells the king,
and he feeds with his own ambrosial food those who dwell (under) him.
Truth rests upon her head.
She expresses joy by (the movement of) her feet.
Her mouth is open, and that becomingly,
+as (with it) she sings loud songs of praise.+
Thirty and two are those who praise her.
Her tongue is like the curtain of the door,
which is flung back by those who enter in.
+Like steps her neck mounts up+,
which the first creator created.
Her two hands make signs and point to the land of the aeons.
Her fingers open the gates of the city.
Her bridal chamber is full of light,
breathing a scent of balsam and all sweet herbs,
it gives out a sweet smell of myrrh and aromatic leaves.
Within are strewn myrtle branches.
The entrances are adorned with reeds.
Her groomsmen keep her compassed about, seven in number,
whom she herself has chosen;
and her bridesmaids are seven,
who dance in rings before her.
Twelve are they in number who serve before her
and are subject to her.
They direct their gaze towards the bridegroom,
that they may be illuminated by the sight of him.

And for ever shall they be with him in that eternal joy.
And they shall be at that marriage
for which the prominent men assemble,
and linger over the feast,
of which the eternal ones are accounted worthy.
And they shall put on royal robes
and be arrayed in splendid garments.
And both shall be in joy and exultation,
and they shall glorify the Father of all,
whose proud light they received.
And they have been illuminated by the gaze of their Lord,
whose ambrosial food they received,
which remains in them undiminished.
They drank too of the wine,
which stirs in them neither thirst nor desire.
They glorified and praised with the living Spirit,
the father of truth and the mother of wisdom.

From the Odes of Solomon

The motif of the wedding, which stands for the union between believers and Saviour, can also be found in the Odes of Solomon. Here, however, the metaphor does not attest a sacramental action as in the Gospel of Philip but is the expression of a religious poetry which comes to a climax in the bridal mysticism.

The beginning of the following hymn is no longer extant.

(OdSol 3)(...) I clothe.
And my members are with him,
and on them I depend and he loves me.
For I would not know how to love the Lord if he did not love me.
Who could choose love,[134] but the one who is loved?
I love the beloved, and my soul loves him.
And where his rest[135] is, (there) too am I.
And I will not be a stranger, because there is no resentment with the Lord, the supreme and merciful one.

I am married,
because the lover found the beloved,
because I should love him, the son, that I might become a son.
For he who is bound up with that one who does not die will also
be immortal.
And he who has pleasure in life will be alive.
That is the spirit of the Lord, who is without falsehood, who
teaches humankind to know his ways.
Be wise and have knowledge and be watchful!
Hallelujah.[136]

Eucharistic prayers

For Christians, alongside baptism the eucharist was the most
important sacramental practice (cf. Ignatius, Smyrn. 7.1; 8.1; Justin,
Apol. I 61). It goes back to Christ's last supper, attested in the New
Testament. The Gnostics, too, knew prayers at meals and eucharistic
prayers, which have either the character of invocations as in the apostolic Acts used among the Gnostics or show markedly magical features
like the Marcosian eucharist or the celebration in the Pistis Sophia. In
particular the magical character of the Gnostic eucharist often led the
church fathers and heresiarchs to engage in defamatory polemic (cf.
below, pp.120f.).

Valentinian eucharist

Although it has been preserved in a fragmentary state, this text is clear
evidence that there were sacraments similar to the eucharist among the
Valentinians.

(NHC XI 2; 43,20ff.) [We give] thanks [to you and we celebrate
the eucharist], Father, [remembering for the sake of] your Son
[Jesus Christ that they] come forth [...] invisible [...] [...] [...]
your [Son...] [...] his [love...] them [...] to [the knowledge] [...]
they are doing your will [now and] always. They are perfect [in]
every grace and [every] purity. [Glory] be to you through your
Son [and] your offspring Jesus Christ, [from now] for ever.
Amen.

Marcosian eucharist

The church father Irenaeus towards the end of the second century reports the Marcosian eucharist at length.

(Irenaeus, *Haer.* I 13, 2) He (viz. Marcus) pretends to say the thanksgiving over a cup mixed with wine, and draws out the word of invocation (epiclesis) to great length. He contrives to give the wine a reddish colour, and one is to believe that the grace which comes from the highest spheres drips her blood into his cup at his invocation, and that those present are eager to taste of this drink, in order that the grace conjured up by this magician may also rain down on them. Or, he gives such mixed cups to the women and bids them say the thanksgiving over them in his presence. When this has been done, he himself then takes another cup which is much larger than that over which the deluded woman has said the thanskgiving, pours the wine from the smaller cup over which the woman has said the thanksgiving into the one which he has brought, and says:

> May the grace which was before all things,
> inconceivable, ineffable,
> fill your inner self
> and multiply in you her knowledge,
> by sowing the grain of mustard seed in the good earth.

Repeating certain other like words, he completely confuses the wretched woman and plays the miracle-worker, as the larger cup becomes so full from the smaller one that it overflows. With just such things he has deceived many, and bound them to him.

From the Acts of Thomas I

The eucharistic prayers from the Acts of Thomas always have the character of invocations. They are not explicitly Gnostic in content, but like the whole of the Acts of Thomas were used by the Gnostics. Because the Acts were held in high esteem among the Gnostics and are often influenced by Gnosticism, we may assume that the prayers contained in them were also an ingredient of Gnostic piety.[137]

(Acts of Thomas 50) +Come, gift of the Most High!+
Come, perfect compassion!
Come, fellowship with the male!
+Come, Holy Spirit (power)!+
Come, knower of the mysteries of the chosen!
Come, participant in all the combats of the noble fighter (athlete)!
+Come, treasure of glory!
Come, darling of the mercy of the Most High!+
Come, silence, you who reveal the mighty deeds of the whole greatness!
Come, you who unveil the hidden things and make the secret manifest!
+Come+, holy dove, you who bore the twin young!
Come, hidden Mother!
Come, you who are manifest through your deeds and give joy and rest to all that are joined with you!
Come and partake with us in this eucharist
which we celebrate in your name,
and in the love feast at which we are gathered together at your invitation.

From the Acts of Thomas II

(Acts of Thomas 133) Bread of life, those who eat of which are to remain incorruptible;
bread, which fills hungry souls with its blessing – you are the one who has been thought worthy to receive a gift, so that you become for us forgiveness of sins and those who eat of you become immortal.
We name over you the name of the Mother of the cryptic mystery of the hidden rules and authorities.
We name over you the name of Jesus.
(...)
May the power of blessing come and descend upon the bread, that all souls which partake of it are washed from their sins.

From the Acts of Thomas III

(Acts of Thomas 158) Your holy body which was crucified for us we eat, and your blood which was shed for us for salvation we drink. May your body now become for us salvation, and your blood (serve) for the forgiveness of sins!
And for the gall which you drank for our sakes, may the gall of the devil around us be taken away.
And for the vinegar which you drank for us, our weakness will be strengthened.
And for the spitting which you received for our sake, let us receive the dew of your goodness.
And because of the reed with which they struck you for our sake, let us receive the perfect house.
Because you received the crown of thorns for our sake, let us who have loved you be girded with a crown that does not fade away.
And for the linen cloth in which you were wrapped, let us be girded with your unconquerable power.
And for the new tomb and burial, let us receive renewal of soul and body.
And because you rose and came to life again, let us come to life again and live and stand before you in righteous judgment.

From the Acts of John

Eucharistic prayers in the form of invocations are also attested in the Acts of John (85; 108). As in the Acts of Thomas they are built into the actions, but originally they could possibly have been independent liturgical texts. Lists which give Christ constantly new designations and titles occur frequently in the apocryphal and Gnostic literature (cf. above, pp.71,76f.).

The following prayer represents a thanksgiving in the context of the eucharist.

(Acts of John 109) What praise and what offering or what thanksgiving shall we name as we break this bread, but you alone, Jesus?

We praise your name of Father which was spoken by you.
We praise your name of Son which was spoken by you.
We praise your entering (given in) the door.
We praise your resurrection shown to us through you.
We praise your way.
We praise your seed,
the word,
the grace,
the faith,
the salt,
the inexpressible pearl,
the treasure,
the plough,
the net,
the greatness,
the diadem,
the one who for our sake was called Son of Man,
the truth, given to us,
the rest,
the knowledge,
the power,
the commandment,
the freedom of speech,
the hope,
the love,
the liberty,
the refuge in you.
For you alone, Lord, are the root of immortality and the fount
of incorruption and the seat of the aeons, you who have been
called all these things on our account, so that we, when we
name you through them, may know your greatness, which at
present is invisible to us, but can be seen only by the pure as it
is portrayed only in your humanity.

Eucharist in the Pistis Sophia

The rituals in the Pistis Sophia, which have a parallel in the Second Book of Jeu, 45ff., are sacramental practices which serve for the forgiveness of sins and bring about entry into the world of light. There are similarities with early Christian eucharistic festivals; thus in both we can detect the offering of gifts, a litany and an invocation.

(Chapters 141ff.)(...) Jesus said to his disciples: 'Approach me!' And they approached him. He turned to the four corners of the world. He said the great name over their heads, he blessed them, he breathed into their eyes. Jesus said to them: 'Look up and see what you see!' And they raised their eyes and saw a great, very powerful light, about which no man of earth can speak.

He spoke again to them: 'Look away from the light and see what you see!' They said: 'We see fire and water and wine and blood.' Jesus, who is Aberamentho,[138] said to his disciples: 'Truly I say to you: When I came, I brought nothing into the world but this fire and this water and this wine and this blood. I have brought the water and the fire from the place of the light of the lights of the treasury of light; I have brought the wine and the blood from the place of the Barbelo. And after a little while my Father sent me the Holy Spirit in the type of a dove. Now the fire, the water and the wine came into being to purify all the sins of the world. But the blood became a sign for me concerning the human body which I received in the place of the Barbelo, the great power of the invisible God. However, the spirit draws all souls together and leads them to the place of light.

Therefore I have said to you: "I have come to cast fire on this world."[139] That means: I have come to purify the sins of the whole world with fire. And for that reason I said to the Samaritan woman: "If you had known the gift of God and who it is that says to you, 'Give me something to drink,' you would have asked him, and he would have given you living water, and it would have become in you a spring *of water*, which springs up to eternal life."[140]

And that is why I also took a cup of wine, blessed it and gave it to them and said: "This is the blood of the covenant which will be shed for you for the forgiveness of your sins."[141] And that is why they also thrust the spear into my side, and water and blood came forth.[142] Now these are the mysteries of the light which forgive sins, that means, the invocations and the names of the light.'

(A short dialogue between Jesus and his disciples follows.)

Now Jesus said to them: 'Bring me fire and vine branches.' They brought them to him; he lifted up the offering and placed two pitchers of wine, one on the right and the other on the left of the offering. He placed the offering in front of them. He placed a cup of water in front of the pitcher of wine which was on the right. And he placed a cup of wine in front of the pitcher which was on the left. And he placed loaves according to the number of the disciples between the cups and put a cup full of water behind the loaves.

Jesus stood before the sacrifice; he placed the disciples behind him, all clothed in linen garments, and in their hands was the stone of the name of the father of the treasury of light. So he cried out, saying:

'Hear me, my Father, you Father of all fatherhood, you infinite light *(magical formulae follow)* – of heaven *(Amen, Amen and magical formulae then alternate).*

Hear me, my Father, you Father of all fatherhood!
I call upon you also,
you forgivers of sins, you purifiers of lawlessnesses.
Forgive the sins of the souls of these disciples
who have followed me,
and purify their lawlessnesses.
Make them worthy to be reckoned
in the kingdom of my Father, the Father of the treasury of light,
for they have followed me and have observed my commandments.
And now, my Father, you Father of all fatherhood,

may the forgivers of sins come, whose names are these: (*magical formulae follow*).

Hear me as I call upon you.
Forgive the sins of these souls and blot out their lawlessnesses.
Make them to be worthy to be reckoned in the kingdom of my Father, the father of the treasury of light.
For I know your great powers and I call upon them: (*magical formulae follow*).

Forgive the sins of these souls and blot out their lawlessnesses which they have committed knowingly and unknowingly!
Forgive them these (lawlessnesses) which they have committed in fornication and adultery to the present day.
  Make them worthy to be reckoned in the kingdom of my Father, so that they are worthy to partake of this offering.
My holy Father, if now, my Father, you have heard me, and you have forgiven the sins of these souls and you have blotted out their lawlessnesses, and you have made them worthy to be reckoned in your kingdom, grant me a sign in this offering.'

And the sign that Jesus had asked for took place. Jesus said to his disciples: 'Rejoice and be glad, for your sins are forgiven and your lawlessnesses are blotted out, and you will be reckoned in the kingdom of my Father.'
(...)
'This now is the true mystery of the baptism of those whose sins will be forgiven and whose lawlessnesses are covered. This is the baptism of the first offering which leads to the place of truth and to the place of light.'

Thereupon his disciples said to him: 'Rabbi, reveal to us the mystery of the light of your Father, as we heard you saying: "There is yet one baptism of fire,[143] and there is another baptism of the Holy Spirit of light and there is a spiritual anointing; these lead the souls to the treasury of light." Now tell us their mystery, that we ourselves may inherit the kingdom of your Father.' Jesus said to them: 'There is no mystery which is more excellent than these mysteries about which you ask, which will lead your souls to the light of lights, to the places of the truth and of goodness, to the place of the holy of all holies, to the place in which there is neither man nor woman,[144] nor are there forms at that place, but a constant, indescribable light.'

Thanksgivings

There are a variety of testimonies in which the Gnostics express their thanks for their salvation or praise the souls which have been saved.

From the Manichaean Psalms of the Wanderer

A Manichaean psalm from the Psalms of the Wanderer describes the state of the redeemed soul. Here we have an expression of the typically Gnostic questing religious feeling.[145]

(MPB II 167,65ff.) I sought, I [found...].
I found the haven.
The haven is the commandment.
I [set] my feet on the path.
The path is the knowledge of God.
I found the ships.
The ships are the sun and the moon.
They carried me over to my city.
I found a profit [in which] there is no loss.
[...]
I found a rest in which there is no toil.
I found a joy in which there is no grief.
I rejoice, I rejoice!
In all eternity!
Give me also the victory, I, the soul of Mary![146]

From the Authentikos Logos

At the end of the Authentikos Logos (NHC VI 3), a tractate whose theme, like that of the Exegesis of the Soul (NHC II 6, pp.129f.), is the fate of the soul, there is a hymn to the soul. Almost in analogy to the Naassene Psalm (see above, pp.50f.), the first part of the hymn depicts the fate of the soul in the world and the way from the world, the second part the salvation which is encountered. The salvation of the soul consists in its quest for knowledge – fully in accord with the Gnostic religion of seeking; here its deliverance from the world consists in 'repose', the supreme eschatological saving good.

(NHC VI 3; 34,32ff.): Now the mindful soul,
which toiled in her quest,
received knowledge about God.
She tormented herself
by enquiring,
by suffering in her body,
by wearing out her feet after the evangelists,[147]
by receiving knowledge about the Inscrutable One.

She found her ascent.
She came to rest in him who is at rest.
She lay down in the bridal chamber.
She ate of the banquet for which she had longed.
She partook of the immortal food.
She found what she had sought.
She received rest from her labours, since the light shines upon her which does not fade.

From the Pistis Sophia

The following hymn is a thanksgiving by the redeemed Pistis Sophia to her Saviour (see above). There are many such attestations of thanks in chs. 68–76, which like the lamentations in 32–57 are interpreted by the disciples of Jesus.

(Chapter 68) I have been delivered from chaos.
And I have been freed from the fetters of darkness.
I have come to you, light.

For you have become light on all sides of me, since you have
saved me and since you have helped me.
And you have hindered through your light
the emanations of Authades
– those who rose up against me.
And they were not able to approach me,
for your light was with me.
And you have delivered me through your outpouring of light.
For when the emanations of Authades oppressed me,
they took my power from me,
they cast me into the chaos (plural) in which no light is.
I became as heavy matter before them.
And after these things an outpouring power came over me from
you, delivering me.
It made my left hand and my right hand light,
and it surrounded me on all sides, so that no part of me was
without light.
And you have clothed me with the light of your outpouring,
and you have purified me from all evil matter.
And I have been raised above all my matter because of your
light.
And your outpouring of light is what has raised me up.
And he has taken away from me the emanations of Authades
which tormented me,
and in your light I took courage and I became a pure light of
your outpouring.
And the emanations of the Authades which oppressed me have
departed far from me.
And I became light in your great power, for you have saved me
for ever.

A Gnostic hymn of thanksgiving

This hymn of thanksgiving from the Odes of Solomon gives an
example of the spirituality of Syrian Gnostic Christians in the second
and third century CE.

(OdSol 21) I have raised my arms on high
to the mercy of the Lord;
for he has cast off my fetters from me.
And my helper has raised me up
to his mercy and to his salvation.
And I have put off the darkness
and clothed myself in the light.
And there became members in my soul
in which is no pain nor any torment nor suffering.
And the thought of the Lord was abundantly helpful to me
and his indestructible fellowship.
And I was taken on high by the light
and went over into his presence.
And I was near to him
while I praised and confessed him.
He made my heart spring forth
and he was in my mind and arose upon my lips.
And great upon my countenance became
the jubilation of the Lord in his glory.
Hallelujah.[148]

Mandaean praise of the soul

There is praise by the saved soul both in the Left Ginza and in the
Mandaean Liturgies. This text is part of the Mandaean mass of the
dead (Masiqta).

(LG II 3; 78 and ML Qolasta XCIV; 159f.)
Hail to you, hail to you, soul, for you have left the world.
You have forsaken decay
and the stinking body in which you dwelt,
the abode, the abode of the evil ones,
the place which is full of sinners,
the world of darkness,
of hatred, envy and malice,
the abode in which the planets dwell
which bring pain and affliction.
They bring pain and affliction

and daily they provoke disturbance.
Arise, arise, soul,
ascend to your former land.
To your former land ascend,
to the place from which you were planted,
to the place which you were planted from,
to your good abode of the powers.[149]
Arise, put on your garment of splendour
and put on your glorious crown.
Sit on your throne of splendour
which life has established in the place of light.
Arise, dwell in the heavenly places,[150]
between the powers, your brothers.
As you have been accustomed,
bless your primal home
and curse this place
of the house of your foster-father.
For the years that you spent in it
were the seven your opponents.
Your opponents were the seven,
and the twelve were your persecutors.
Life is upheld and is victorious,
and victorious is the man who has gone here.[151]

A Hermetic prayer

The following Gnostic prayer has been preserved in many places; not only is it to be found among the Nag Hammadi writings (NHC VI 7a), but a Greek and a Latin version also exist.[152] The prayer is a thanksgiving and indicates the cultic practice of the Hermetic community. That seems probable not only because of the liturgical character of the writing but also because the note immediately attached to the prayer, that those taking part kiss one another and partake in a holy, liturgical meal, is a reference to the Hermetic cult.

That is the prayer that they said:
'We thank you:
Every soul and (every) heart is lifted up to you,

(you) name which is not disturbed,
which is honoured by the name "God"
and which is praised by the name "Father".
For to each one and to the All (comes) the kindness of the Father,
the good will and the love,
and any teaching there may be which is sweet and plain and gives us mind, word (and) knowledge:
mind, that we may understand you,
word, that we may explain you,
and knowledge, that we may know you.

We rejoice: we have been enlightened by your knowledge.
We rejoice: you have shown yourself to us.
We rejoice: while we are in (the) body, you have divinized us by your knowledge.

The thanks of the man who attains to you is one thing: that we (can) know you.
We have known you, O mindful light.
O life of life, we have known you.
O womb of every creature, we have known you.
O womb which gives birth through the nature of the Father, we have known you.
O eternal permanence of the begetting Father, thus we have revered your goodness.

There is only one wish that we express: that we may continue to be preserved through knowledge.
And there is one protection for which we ask: that we do not stumble in this kind of life.'

After they had said these things in prayer they kissed one another and went to eat their holy, bloodless food.

The salvation of Norea: an example

The Ode on Norea (NHC IX 2) is a Sethian writing.[153] Thus the divine triad 'Father, Mother, Son' is a characteristic of Sethian Gnosticism, and the four holy helpers (28, 27–28) are in all probability to be identified with the Sethian enlighteners Hamozel, Oroiael, Daveithe and Eleleth.

In form, the 'Ode on Norea' is a hymn-like text, as is already evident from the parallel formulation (cf. 28,1–12).

The writing can be divided into four parts: 1. invocation of the divine triad by Norea (27,11–22); 2. by her prayer Norea again becomes part of the divine world (27,22–28, 12); 3. the redeemed Norea becomes the Saviour by proclaiming 'words of life' (28, 12–23); 4. Norea has the 'four holy helpers' as intercessors with the Father (28,24–29,5).

The 'Ode on Norea' relates the story of a typically Gnostic salvation. After Norea's calls for help, her Saviour comes from the heavenly world. She receives what has always belonged to her and is again united with all the indestructibles. Norea, thus saved, in turn becomes the Saviour by proclaiming the words of life.

(1) (NHC IX 2; 27,11ff.) Father of the All,
[thought (Ennoia)] of the light,
mind, [dwelling] in the heights above the (regions) below,
light, dwelling [in the] heights,
voice of the truth,
upright mind,
untouchable word,
and [ineffable] voice,
[incomprehensible Father]!'

It is Norea who [cries out] to them.

(2) They [heard], (and) they received her into her place for ever. They gave to her the Father of mind, Adama, as well as the voice of the Holy Ones,

that she might rest in the ineffable thought (Epinoia),
that *she* might inherit the original mind which *she* had received,
and (that) *she* might rest in the divine Autogenes,
and (that) she (too) might bring herself forth, just as [she] also has inherited the [living] word,
and (that) she might be united with all the Indestructible Ones,
and [speak] with the mind of the Father.

3. And [she began] to speak with words of [life],
and *she* remained before the [face] of the Most High, [possessing that] which she had received before the world had come into being. [She has] the [great mind] of the Invisible One, [and] [she gives] glory to *her* Father,
[and she] dwells within those who [...] [...] in the Pleroma,
[and] she beholds the Pleroma.

4. There will be days when she will [behold] the Pleroma, and she will not be in deficiency, for she has the four holy helpers who mediate on her behalf with the Father of the All, Adama. He is within all of the Adamites who possess the thought of Norea, who speaks about the two names which produce a single name.

4

Hostility from the Church

The church Christians did not understand the indefatigable striving of the Gnostics for a higher truth, their questing religion, and even saw it as a danger. So the documents of Gnostic spirituality and the testimonies to the liturgical actions of the Gnostics were suppressed and defamed. In particular the Gnostic rituals and sacraments fell victim to the polemic of the mainstream church. Here the high esteem in which women were held in the Gnostic cult and in Gnostic teaching was the occasion for sharp criticism.[154]

The defaming of the cult

As an example of the defaming of the Gnostic cult by the catholic church Christians and heresiologists, here first is the polemic of Epiphanius of Salamis against the eucharistic celebrations of the Phibionites (*Haer*. 26, 4f.) and the Ophites (*Haer*. 37, 5f.). The wicked (often sexual) acts imputed to the Gnostics by Epiphanius ironically have points of similarity with the charges which were made against (catholic!) Christians in the persecutions of Christians during the second and third centuries.[155] Thus in his defence entitled *Octavius* (c.200), the Christian apologist Minucius Felix sums up the prejudices of the opponents of Christianity (*Octavius* 9). He quotes the orator M. Cornelius Fronto, the teacher of Marcus Aurelius, who evidently delivered and published a speech against the Christians.

Defaming of the Gnostic cult by church Christians

(Epiphanius, *Haer*. 26, 4, 1ff.) (...)They favour the abundant enjoyment of feasting and drinking wine, even if they are poor (...). And the husband will withdraw from his wife in order to say to her – his own wife – 'Arise, make agape (= love) with your brother.' (...) And the wretches mingle (...) The woman and the man take the efflux of the male (=sperm) in their hands. They come forward, raise their eyes to heaven and pray, bearing the uncleanness in their hands (...) 'We offer you this gift, the body of Christ.' (...) And so they eat it and communicate their own shame and say: 'That is the body of Christ, and that is the Pasch on account of which our bodies suffer and are compelled to confess the passion of Christ.' And (they act) similarly with the (blood) of the woman. When the woman has her period, the monthly blood of her uncleanness which issues from her is collected and similarly they eat it together. And they say, 'That is the blood of Christ.'

(Epiphanius, *Haer.* 37, 5, 1ff.) (...) They pile loaves of bread upon a table. They summon the snake. When the container is opened, it emerges (...) and comes on to the table and moves around among the loaves (....) and that they call the perfect sacrifice. (...) They break the loaves around which the snake has moved and give them to the communicants. Each one kisses the snake on the mouth, as the snake has been tamed by conjurations (...) They prostrate themselves before such a beast (...) Through it (viz. the snake), they send up, as they say, a hymn to the Father above. So they perfect their mysteries.

Defaming of the Christian cult by non-Christians

(Minucius Felix, *Octavius* 9.5) Now the story about the initiation of new members is as abhorrent as it is well known. A child covered with dough to deceive the unwary is placed before the one to be initiated. This child is killed by the novice with wounds which completely escape the eye; he himself mistakenly thinks that the thrusts through the covering of dough are harmless. They greedily lick up the blood of the child – what a sacrilege! – truly competing over its dismemberment. By this sacrifice they become brothers. With this complicity in such a crime they guarantee one another mutual silence (...)

(9.6) Their feastings are also well known. People speak of them everywhere; even our own Cirtensian[156] testifies to them in his discussion. On a solemn day they assemble for the feast with all their children, sisters, mothers, people of every sex and age. When the company is heated after a rich meal and the fervour of impure lust is made hot by drunkenness, a dog that has been tied to the lampstand is provoked to spring forward vigorously, by being thrown pieces of meat which are beyond the length of the cord by which it is tied. Thus the treacherous light is over-turned. Now the bonds of unspeakable passion entangle them in the darkness which encourages shamelessness, as chance disposes (...)[157]

Taunt song aimed at Marcus

The Gnostic Marcus, a disciple of Valentinus, is the representative of a Gnosticism which was strongly stamped by sacraments. Because of the emphasis on ritual practices and a marked speculation involving numbers and letters, he was also given the nickname 'the magician'.[158]

(Irenaeus, *Haer.* I 15, 6) Marcus, you former of idols and inter-preter of portents,
expert in astrology and in magic.
By it you confirm your teachings of errors,
performing signs before the eyes of those whom you have already led astray,
the enterprises of the fallen power,
for which Satan, your father, always equips you,
to perform through the angelic power of Azazel,[159]
as in you he has a precursor in ungodly evil.

Polemic against Egypt

The spiritual climate of Alexandria was an ideal breeding ground for Gnostic thought:[160] the important Gnostic Valentinus presumably comes from Alexandria (cf. Epiphanius, *Haer.* 31, 2, 2f.); the Gnostic Basilides was also active there at the time of the emperor Hadrian (cf.

Irenaeus, *Haer.* I 24, 1).[161] There is a letter by the emperor Hadrian (117–138) about the religious climate in Roman Egypt of which Alexandria was the capital; in all probability it is inauthentic, but nevertheless it is important for assessing the religious situation in Egypt in the second century. The historian Flavius Vopiscus quotes this letter of the emperor Hadrian in the context of his own polemic against Egypt.[162] Here too – as in the reports by the church fathers – the polemic against the creativity of particular religious groups is clear.

(Flav. Vop. VIII) Hadrian Augustus sends his greetings to the consul Servianus! I have come to know Egypt, which you have so praised to me, my dear Servianus, as a quite frivolous land, vacillating and resorting to every piece of gossip. Here those who worship Serapis are Christians, and those who call themselves Christian bishops serve Serapis. Here there is no Jewish synagogue president, no Samaritan, no Christian presbyter, who is not at the same time an astrologer, a soothsayer and a charlatan. If the patriarch himself came to Egypt he would be forced by one of these to worship Serapis and by another to worship Christ. (...) The one god that they have is no god. The Christians worship him, the Jews worship him, and all other peoples worship him.[163]

Additional Material

On the Unknown Father

From the Tripartite Tractate

The Tripartite Tractate (NHC I 5), one of the most extensive and most significant of the Nag Hammadi writings, was not known before the Nag Hammadi discoveries. This text is a 'Gnostic dogmatic' from the Valentinian school;[164] the work has no title, but a division into three parts can be recognized in the codex, hence the name 'Tripartite Tractate'. The individual parts are separated by lines of arrows in the text, which probably served as decoration. The first part is about the Unknown Father, the structure of the Pleroma, the fall and penance of the Logos and the origin of the Pleroma (51,3–104,3); the second part is about the creation of human beings (104,4–108,12); the third part describes, among other things, the activity of the incarnate Saviour which culminates in the restoration of the Pleroma (108,13–138,27). The teaching which is given in the Tripartite Tractate attests a very close combination of Gnosticism and catholic Christianity. Thus for example the abrupt dualism which can be found among the Mandaeans and Manichaeans is replaced by a monism: everything emanates from the good, unknown Father, and even the fall of the Logos[165] takes place in accordance with his will.[166]

Further approximations to the teaching of the church Christians are, for example, the way in which an abrupt anthropological dualism is broken through, and the renunciation of the kind of protest exegesis of the Old Testament with reference to Gen. 1–3 which is customary in Gnosticism. Nor is the depiction of the demiurge as negative as in other Gnostic texts: he is the instrument of the Logos.

Both the theological position between Gnosticism and church Christianity and the proximity to Alexandrian theology suggest a time of composition at the end of the second or beginning of the third centuries. It looks as if the Gnostics standing behind the Tripartite

Tractate had attempted to go into the questions raised by the church Christians and to develop draft solutions.

What make this tractate interesting for the Gnostic practice of piety are the numerous hymnic sections, which perhaps go back to earlier tradition (cf. pp. 71,142ff.).

(NHC I 5; 51.3ff.) As for what we can say about the exalted things, it is fitting to begin with the Father, who is the root of the All, the one from whom we have received grace (to be able) to say something about him.

He existed before anything other than himself came into being. The Father alone is a single one, like a number, for he is the first and the one who is only himself, in that he is not like any solitary individual. Otherwise, how could he be a father? For wherever there is a 'father', the name 'son' follows.

But the single one who alone is the Father is like a root with a tree, branches and fruit. It is said of him that he is a father in the proper sense, since he is inimitable and immutable. Because of this he is single in the proper sense and is a god, because no one (else) is a god for him, nor is there anyone who is a father to him. For he is unbegotten, and there is no other who begot him, nor another who created him. For whoever is someone's father or his creator, (for his part) also has a father and creator (...).

He is without beginning and he is without end. He is not only without end – he is immortal for this reason, that he is unbegotten – but he is also unshakeable in his eternal existence and in his identity and in that by which he stands fast and in that by which he is great. Neither will he withdraw from that by which he is, nor will anything else force him to produce an end which he has never desired. He has had no one who made a beginning of his own existence. Thus, he is himself unchangeable and no one else is able to withdraw him from his existence and his identity, in which he is, and his greatness, so that he cannot be taken away;

nor is it possible for anyone else to change him into a different form

or to reduce him

or alter him
or diminish him.
For this is so in the proper sense of his kind: he is the
unalterable, immutable one, with immutability clothing him.

Not only is he the one of whom they say, '(He is) without
beginning' and '(He is) without end', for he is unbegotten and
immortal; but just as he has no beginning and no end, in the
kind that he is, he is
unsurpassable in his greatness,
inscrutable in his wisdom,
incomprehensible in his power,
unfathomable in his sweetness.

In the proper sense he is alone – the good, the unbegotten
Father and the one who is completely without lack – the one
who is full of all his offspring and of every virtue and of
everything that is of value (...)

He is of such a kind and form and great magnitude that no
one else was with him from the beginning;
nor is there any place in which he is, or from which he has come
forth, or into which he will go;
nor is there any first form which he uses as a model as he works,
nor is there any difficulty which is his in that it follows him in
what he does;
nor is there any material which is at his disposal, through which
he creates what he creates;
nor any substance within him from which he begets what he
begets;
nor any co-worker in him, who works with him on the things
on which he works.
To say anything of this sort shows ignorance. But (one should
speak of him) as 'good' (and) 'faultless',
in that he is perfect,
in that he is full,
in that he is himself the All.

For none of the names which are conceived with the mind, or
spoken, or seen, or grasped, none of them applies to him, even
though they are exceedingly glorious, magnifying and honoured.

But it is possible to use these names for his glory and honour, in accordance with the capacity of each of those who give him glory. But as for him, as he exists, as he is, and as the form in which he is,
neither will mind be able to understand him,
nor will any speech be able to convey him,
nor will any eye be able to see him,
nor will any body be able to grasp him,
because of his unfathomable greatness
and his incomprehensible depth,
and his immeasurable height,
and his illimitable will.

This is the nature of the unbegotten one, who does not touch anything else, nor is he joined (to anything) in the manner of something which is determined. But he possesses this constitution, in that he has neither a face nor a form, things which are known through perception, whence also comes (the epithet) 'the incomprehensible'. If he is incomprehensible, then it follows
that he cannot be grasped by the mind,
that he is inconceivable by any mind,
invisible by any thing,
unutterable by any word,
untouchable by any hand.

He alone is the one who knows himself as he is,
with his form and his greatness and his stature,
and (only) he has the ability
to understand himself,
to see himself,
to name himself,
to comprehend himself,
he alone is the one who is his own mind,
his own eye,
his own mouth,
his own form,
and he is what he thinks,
what he sees,

what he speaks,
what he grasps,
himself, the one who is inconceivable,
unutterable,
incomprehensible,
immutable,
whereby he is nourishment,
whereby he is delight,
whereby he is truth,
whereby he is joy,
whereby he is rest (for what) he comprehends,
what he sees,
what he says,
what he has as thoughts.
He transcends all wisdom,
and he towers above all mind,
and he towers above all glory,
and he towers above all beauty,
and all sweetness,
and all greatness,
and all depth
and all height.
If this one, who is unknowable in his nature, to whom belong
all the greatnesses which I have already mentioned, if out of the
depth of his sweetness he wishes to grant knowledge so that he
may be known, he has the ability to do so. He has his power,
which is his will. Now, however, in silence he himself holds
back, he who is the great one, who is the cause of the bringing
forth of the allnesses into their eternal existence. (...)
That which is worthy of his admiration and glory and honour
and praise, he brings forth because of the boundlessness of his
greatness,
and the unsearchability of his wisdom,
and the immeasurability of his power
and his untastable sweetness.
(...)

On the fate of the soul

The Exegesis of the Soul

The Exegesis of the Soul (NHC II 6)[167] depicts the fall and the deliverance of the soul: the soul leaves her true bridegroom and devotes herself to earthly fornication with adulterers (127,18ff.). However, she recognizes her misbehaviour and wants to return to her true bridegroom (131,18ff.; 135,21: 'For repentance is the beginning of salvation.'). After the soul has purified herself from her former sins (131,34ff.: 'Now the purification of the soul (consists in) her receiving the [newness] of her original nature, and returning to herself again – this is her baptism.'), she unites herself again with her true bridegroom and conceives children by him (134,13ff.: 'This is the resurrection from the dead. This is salvation from captivity. This is the ascent to heaven. This is the way to the Father.'). The fate of the fallen and saved soul is like that of Helen, the consort of Simon Magus (Irenaeus, *Haer.* I 23, 2f.):

(2f.) (...) He carried around with him a certain woman named Helena, whom he had ransomed from prostitution in Tyre, a Phoenician city, and said that this woman was his 'first thought' (first Ennoia), the mother of all, by whom in the beginning he conceived in his mind to create angels and archangels. This Ennoia, which sprang forth from him, comprehending the will of her father, descended below and gave birth to angels and powers, by whom according to him this world was also made. But after she had given birth to them, she was detained by them out of envy, because they did not want to be looked upon as the progeny of any other being. For he himself had remained totally unknown to them; but his Ennoia was detained by those powers and angels which had gone forth from her and suffered all kinds of shame from them, so that she could not return again to her father. So much so that she was shut up in a human body, and through the centuries passed in succession from one female body to another, as from vessel to vessel. She was, for example, in that Helen on whose account the Trojan war was begun, for whose sake also Stesichorus, who had shamed her in a poem, was deprived of the sight of his eyes; afterwards he had been sorry and wrote what are called palinodes in praise of her, and so he regained his sight. Thus she, passing from body to body, and suffering insults in every one of them, at last found herself in a brothel – and she was the lost sheep. For this purpose, then, he had come that he might take her first, and free her from her fetters, and confer salvation upon men, that they might know themselves. (...)[168]

The model for the myth of the soul in the Exegesis of the Soul is probably the Gnostic (pre-Valentinian) Sophia myth; within the Nag Hammadi writings the Exegesis of the Soul shows similarities especially to the Gospel of Philip and the Gospel of Thomas (androgynous myth, bridal sacrament). There are also many parallels to the Authentikos Logos (NHC VI 3) in connection with the fate of the soul. In the Exegesis of the Soul, the heavenly Father is identical with the god of the Old Testament, a standpoint unusual for Gnosticism, though it is also developed in the Authentikos Logos and the Teachings of Silvanus.

The great length of the quotations, most of which come from the Old Testament (Psalms; Prophets), is striking. However, texts are also taken from the New Testament (above all Paul), the Apostolic Fathers (I Clement) and Homer. It is possible that the author is taking these from already existing collections of quotations (florilegia) which possibly already had a Gnostic colouring. The function of the quotations is to point to the narrative of the fall and the salvation of the soul already contained in the holy scriptures (OT/NT) and old, true, credible witnesses (Homer).

The dating of the writing fluctuates between a very early time of origin (archaic myth; no extensive mythological system) and a very late date of origin (deliberately simplified myth). Not only the dating but also the unity of the writing is much disputed: do we have a complicated literary-critical process (quotations = redaction) or should we assume that the writing is a relative unity (quotations = the original ingredients of the writing)?

The literary form of the Exegesis of the Soul is difficult to define; at all events it has novel features. It is striking that each subject division (fall, repentance, deliverance) is commented on with a sentence (cf. above). However, the paraenetic character of the work emerges clearly. The fate of the soul is depicted so that the readers are also moved to repentance and to achieve salvation (perhaps through sacramental actions: baptism/bridal chamber: 137,23ff. 'If we truly repent, God will hear us.'). The fact that the Exegesis of the Soul represents something like a 'conversion work' and has a missionary character could also explain the archaic structure of the Gnostic myth of the soul: a developed mythological system as for example in the Paraphrase of Shem (NHC VII 1) would hardly attract people because of its esoteric and therefore fundamentally incomprehensible basic standpoint. By contrast, with its clear structure the esoteric writing Exegesis of the Soul explains the Gnostic doctrine of salvation to people of late antiquity against the background of Middle-Platonic Wisdom teaching. The religious truth of this doctrine of salvation is proved by the quotation of old, familiar and even holy writings.

The conversion character of the work also emerges clearly: the last paragraph (137,23ff.) could even suggest a liturgical use.

(NHC II 6; 127,19ff.) The wise men who lived before us gave the soul a feminine name. In fact she is a female in her nature as well. She has her womb likewise (like other women). As long as she was alone with the Father, she was a virgin and androgynous in form. But when she had fallen down into a body and had come into this life, she fell into the hands of many robbers. And the wicked ones passed her from one to another and [violated her]. Some abused her [by force], while others (acted in such a way that they) persuaded her with [a] misleading gift. In short, she was violated, and she [lost her] virginity.

And with her body she prostituted herself and gave herself to everyone, because she thought that each one she was about to embrace was her (legitimate) husband. Each time she had given herself to the wanton, unfaithful adulterers, so that they (could) abuse her, she sighed deeply and repented. But even when she turns her face from these adulterers, she tends to run to others; and they compel her to live with them and serve them on their bed, as if they were her masters. Yet for shame she no longer dares to leave them. But they (the adulterers) deceive her for a long time, pretending to her that they are faithful, true husbands, as if they greatly respected her. And after all this they abandon her and go (away).

She then tends to become a poor desolate widow, without help; nor does she have anyone who hears her in her sorrow; for she had received nothing from them except the violations they had done to her when they had sexual intercourse with her. And those (children) which she produced by the adulterers are dumb, blind and sick. Their (the children's) understanding is confused.

But when the Father who is in heaven above seeks her and looks down upon her and sees her sighing – with her sufferings and disgrace – and how she repents of the fornication in which she engaged, and how she is beginning to call upon [his name], so that he may help her, [crying] with all her heart and saying, 'Save me, my Father, for behold I will give an account [to you], [for I abandoned] my house and fled from my maiden's quarters! Take me back to yourself again,' – and when he sees her in such a state, then in his mercy he will count her worthy; for many are the pains which have come upon her, because she has abandoned her house.

Now the Holy Spirit prophesies about the fornication of the soul in many places. For he says in the prophet Jeremiah: 'If the husband casts out his wife, and she goes and takes another man, can she return to him after that? Has not that woman utterly defiled herself? And you have committed fornication with many shepherds, and you returned to me,' says the Lord. 'Lift up your eyes on high and see (the place) where you fornicated. Did you not sit in the streets defiling the land with your unchaste acts and your vices? And you took many shepherds – to your own disaster. You became shameless to everyone. You did not call on me as householder or as father or guardian of your virginity.'[169]

Again, it is written in the prophet Hosea: 'Come, go to law with your mother, for she will not be my wife, and I will not be her husband. I shall remove her fornication from my presence, and I shall tear her adultery from between her breasts. I shall make her naked as on the day of her birth. And I [shall] make her desolate like a land without [water]. And I shall make her childless [through thirst. I] shall have no mercy on her children, for they are children of fornication, because their mother practised fornication and put [her children to shame]. For she says,

'I shall commit fornication with my lovers, (for) they were the ones who gave me my bread and my water and my garments and my coats and my wine and my oil and everything I needed.' Therefore behold I shall shut them up (viz. her ways: LXX) so that she shall not be able to run after her adulterers. And when she seeks them and does not find them, she will say, 'I shall return to my first husband, for in those days I was better off than now.'[170]

Again he says in Ezekiel: 'It came to pass after many wickednesses, says the Lord, that you built yourself a brothel and you made yourself a beautiful place in the streets. And you built yourself brothels on every way, and you wasted your beauty, and you spread your legs in every alley, and you multiplied your fornication. You fornicated with the sons of Egypt, your neighbours who have great flesh.'[171]

Who are 'the sons of Egypt, who have great flesh', if not fleshly and sensual (matters) and the matters of the earth with which the soul defiled itself here, when it accepted bread from them, when it accepted wine, when it accepted oil, when it accepted clothing, and the other external trinkets which surround the body? These (are all) things which she thinks (could be) useful to her.

But of this fornication the apostles of the Saviour proclaimed, 'Guard yourselves against it, purify yourselves from it.'[172] (Here) they are speaking not only of the fornication of the body but rather of that (viz. fornication) of the soul. [For this reason] the apostles [write to the churches] of God, so that such [things] may not occur among [us]. Yet the greatest [concern] has to do with the fornication of the soul. From it also arises the fornication of the body. Therefore Paul, writing to the Corinthians, says, 'I wrote you in the letter, "Do not associate with prostitutes, and in no way with the prostitutes of this world or the greedy or the thieves or idolaters, since then you would have to go out from the world."'[173] (But) here he is speaking pneumatically: 'For our struggle is not against flesh and blood,' as he says, 'but against the world rulers of this darkness and the spirits of wickedness.'[174]

As long as the soul keeps running to and fro by having sexual intercourse with whomever she meets and defiling herself, she exists in the suffering of her just deserts. But when she perceives the straits she is in, and weeps to the Father and repents, then the Father will have mercy on her; he will make her womb turn (away) from the outside and again turn it inwards, so that the soul receives her proper character. They (viz., the wombs of the soul) are not like women. For the wombs of the body are inside the body like the entrails. But the womb of the soul surrounds the outside like the male genitalia, which are external.

Now when the womb of the soul turns itself inwards, by the will of the Father, it is baptized and it immediately becomes clean from the external pollution which was pressed upon it, just as dirty [garments] are usually put into the [water and] turned (to and fro) until their dirt is removed and they become pure. Now the purification of the soul (consists in) her receiving the [newness] of her original nature and returning to herself again. This is her baptism.

Then she will begin to become angry with herself like a woman in labour who writhes in anger in the hour of delivery.

But since she is a woman, she is not in a position to produce a child by herself. The Father sent her from heaven her husband, who is her brother, the firstborn. Then the bridegroom came down to the bride. She gave up her former fornication, she cleansed herself from the pollutions of the adulterers. Then she renewed herself to be a bride. She cleansed herself in the bridal chamber. She filled it with perfume. She sat in it waiting for the true bridegroom. She no longer ran to the market place, having sexual intercourse with whomever she desired, but she continued to look out for him, (because she did not know) on what day he would come, and she feared him, for she did not know what he looked like. She no longer remembers (him) since the time she fell from her Father's house. But by the will of the Father *...* and she dreamed of him like a woman in love with a man.

But then the bridegroom according to the Father's will came down to her into the bridal chamber, which had been made ready. And he decorated the bridal chamber. For that marriage is not like the fleshly marriage, in which those who are having sexual intercourse with each other tend to achieve satisfaction through that intercourse. And as if it were a burden, they leave behind them the disquiet of desire and they [turn away from] each other.

But that (pneumatic) marriage [is not of this kind]. Rather, when they unite [with each other], they become a single life. That is why the prophet says about the first man and the first woman, 'They will become one flesh.'[175] For in the beginning they were joined to each other in the Father, before the woman abandoned the man, who is her brother. This (pneumatic) marriage has joined them together again. And the soul united with her true love, her natural master, as it is written: 'For the master of the woman is her husband.'[176]

Then gradually she recognized him, and she rejoiced again, weeping before him as she remembered the disgrace of her former widowhood. And she adorned herself still more, so that he might find pleasure in staying with her. And the prophet says in the Psalms: 'Hear, my daughter, and see and incline your ear and forget your people and your father's house, for the king has desired your beauty, for he is your lord.'[177] For he requires her to turn her face from her people and the multitude of her adulterers, in whose midst she once was, to devote herself only to her king, her natural master, and to forget the house of her earthly father, with whom things went badly for her, and to remember her father who is in heaven. Thus again it was said to Abraham, 'Come out from your country and your kinsfolk and from your father's house.'[178]

Thus when the soul [had adorned] herself again in her beauty [...] she met her beloved. And [he also] loved her. And when she had sexual intercourse with him, she received from him the seed – 'that is the life-giving spirit'[179] – so that by him she might bear good children and rear them. For this is the great, perfect marvel of birth.

And so this marriage is made perfect according to the will of the Father. But it is fitting that the soul should regenerate herself and become again as she formerly was. The soul moves of her own accord. And (thereupon) she received the divine nature from the Father for her rejuvenation, so that she (might) be restored to the place where she had been from the beginning. This is the resurrection from the dead. This is the salvation from captivity. This is the ascent to heaven. This is the way up to the Father. Therefore the prophet says: 'Praise the Lord, my soul, and, all that is in me (praise) his holy name. My soul, praise God, who forgave all your transgressions, who healed all your sicknesses, who saved your life from death, who crowned you with mercy, who satisfies your longing with good things. Your youth will be renewed like an eagle's.'¹⁸⁰

Now that she has become young again she will ascend, praising the Father and her brother, by whom she was delivered. Thus the soul will be delivered by rebirth. But this does not come about through ascetic words, nor through arts nor through written learning. Rather [it] is the grace of the [...], rather it is the gift of the [...]. For this is a heavenly matter. Therefore the Saviour exclaimed: 'No one can come to me unless my Father draws him and brings him to me; and I myself will raise him up on the last day.'¹⁸¹

It is therefore fitting to pray to the Father and to call upon him with all our soul – not (only) externally with the lips but with the spirit, which is inward, which came forth from the depths:
sighing;
repenting for the life that we lived;
confessing our sins;
perceiving the vain deception we were in, and the vain zeal;
weeping over how we were in darkness and in the wave;
mourning for ourselves, that he may have pity on us;
hating ourselves for how we are now.

Again the Saviour says, 'Blessed are those who mourn, for they are the ones who will find mercy. Blessed are those who are hungry, for they are the ones who will be filled.'¹⁸² Again he says , 'If anyone does not hate his soul he cannot follow me.'¹⁸³ For repentance is the beginning of salvation. Therefore 'Before Christ's appearance came John, preaching the baptism of repentance.'¹⁸⁴ And repentance takes place in distress and grief.

But the Father is good and loves humanity, and he hears the

soul that calls upon him and sends it the light of salvation. Therefore he says through the spirit of the prophet: 'Say to the sons of my people, "[If your] sins extend [from earth to] heaven, and if they become [redder] than scarlet and blacker than [sackcloth and if] you return to me with all your soul and say to me, 'My father,' I will hear you as a holy people." '[185]

Again (he says in) another place: 'Thus says the Lord, the Holy One of Israel: "If you return and sigh, then you will be saved and will know where you were when you put your trust in what is vanity." '[186]

Again he says in another place: 'Jerusalem wept bitterly, saying, "Have mercy on me." He will have mercy on the sound of your weeping. And when he saw, he heard you. And the Lord will give you bread of affliction and water of oppression. From now on the false leaders will not approach you again. Your eyes will see those who mislead you.'[187]

Therefore it is fitting to pray to God night and day, spreading out our hands towards him as do people in the middle of the sea tossing (in the waves); these pray to God with all their heart without hypocrisy. Those who pray hypocritically deceive themselves. 'For God examines the reins and searches out the heart,'[188] the bottom of the heart, to know who is worthy of salvation. For no one is worthy of salvation who still loves the place of deception. Therefore it is written in the poet: 'Odysseus sat on the island; he wept and grieved and turned his face from the words of Calypso and from her seductions, and he longed to see his village (or at least) smoke rising from it. And had he not [received] help from heaven, [he would not have been able to return] to his village.'[189]

Again [Helen] says: '*....* [my beloved] has turned away from me. I want to go to my house.'[190]

For she sighed and said: 'It is Aphrodite who has deceived me and brought me out of my city. And I have abandoned my firstborn daughter and my good, wise, handsome husband.'[191]

For when the soul leaves her perfect husband because of the deceit of Aphrodite, who exists here in the act of bringing forth, then she (viz. the soul) will suffer harm. But if she sighs and repents, she will be restored to her house. For Israel too would not have been visited in the first place, to be brought out of the land of Egypt, out of the house of servitude, if it had not sighed to God and wept for the burden of its (forced) labour. Again it is written in the Psalms: 'I had become very weary in my grief. I will bathe my bed and my cover each night with my tears. I have become old in the midst of all my enemies. Depart from me, all you who do injustice! For behold, the Lord has heard the cry of my weeping and the Lord has heard my prayer.'[192]

If we truly repent, God will heed us, he who is long-suffering and of great mercy, he to whom glory is due for ever and ever. Amen.

The Exegesis of the Soul.

Mandaean Mass of the Dead (Masiqta)

Alongside baptism, the most important sacrament among the Mandaeans is the ceremony of the ascent of the soul (cf. also above, pp.40f.). The following text illustrates the liberation of the soul after the death of a person.

(RG II, 1; 37,16ff. parallel RG I; 19,3ff.) When a soul is saved from the body and departs, do not weep over it; raise no lamentation and mourning over it and consume no hosts[193] over it. Seas and watercourses (from the beyond) will separate anyone who weeps over a soul. Anyone who rends his garment over it will retain a fault in his garment (on the ascent). Anyone who tears his hair over it will be put in the mountain of darkness. If a soul departs from your midst, let the people hear hymns and liturgies, and teach them that their heart should not fall. Give alms for it and distribute bread for it, and read masses of the dead for it and say prayer and praise for it (and recite) hymns and liturgies (for it). Clothe it with garments and shroud it with shrouds, and pay a ransom and say prayers so that he, the Great One,[194] may be full of mercy[195] over them (viz. the souls).

(RG I; 19, 18–21[196]) Splendour will go before them and light follow them. Messengers of life will be on their right hand and angels of light on their left, and they will be preserved from the guardrooms[197] and the boiling cauldrons.[198]

On salvation

An awakening call from the Gospel of Truth

The Gospel of Truth (NHC I 3[199]) is a homily which is attributed to the Valentinian school. It remains an attractive possibility that the Valentinian Gospel of Truth mentioned by Irenaeus *(Haer.* III 11, 19) is identical with this Nag Hammadi writing.

(NHC I 3; 22,2ff.) Therefore, if one has knowledge, he is from above. If he is called, he hears, he answers and turns to the one who calls him and ascends to him. And he knows in what way he is called. Because he has (the) knowledge, he does the will of the One who has called him; he wishes to please him; he receives rest. The name of the One comes to him. The one who has knowledge in this way knows whence he comes and whither he goes. He knows like someone who was drunk and has been sobered up from his drunkenness (and) has returned to himself, has set in order what is his own.

The bridal chamber in the Gospel of Philip

The Gospel of Philip (NHC II 3) is known only through the Nag Hammadi discovery.[200]

The author of the Gospel of Philip sees himself as a Christian, as e.g. sayings 6 and 59 indicate. The New Testament is also cited (23, 69, etc.). In its theological views the Gospel of Philip is especially close to Valentinianism.[201] The clearest indication of this is the prominent position of the sacrament of the bridal chamber which is known from the Valentinian school of the Marcosians (Irenaeus, *Haer.* I 21, 3).

(Saying 122: 81,34ff.) [No one can] know on what day the [husband] and the wife will have sexual intercourse with each other except the two of them. For to those who have taken a wife, the marriage of the world is a mystery. If the marriage of defilement is (already) hidden, how much more is the undefiled marriage a true mystery? It is not fleshly but pure. It belongs not to the desire but to the will. It belongs not to the darkness or (to the) night, but it belongs to the day and to the light (...).

(Saying 127: 86,4ff.) If anyone becomes a child of the bridal chamber, he will receive the light. If anyone does not receive it while he is in these places (= the world), he will not be able to receive it in the other place. He who receives that light will not be able to be seen, nor will he be able to be detained. And no one will be able to molest such a person even if he lives in the world. And even if he leaves the world he has already received the truth in the images (...).

(Saying 61: 65,1ff.) The forms of the unclean spirits are male and female. The males are those that unite with the souls which go about in a female form. But the females are those which are mingled with those in a male form, through one who was disobedient. And no one shall be able to escape them, since they will detain him if he does not receive a male power and a female power – that is the bridegroom and the bride. Now one receives these from the mirrored bridal chamber. When the foolish women see a male who lives alone, they hurl themselves upon him, and they play with him and defile him. So also the foolish men, when they see a beautiful female who lives alone, they chat to her and violate her, because they wish to defile her. But if they see that the man and his wife are living together, the female cannot go to the male, nor can the male go to the female. That is also the case if the image and the angel are united with one another. No one will venture to go to the male or to the female (...).

Ritual of ascent from the Trimorphic Protennoia

As in Zostrianos (see above, pp.94f.), in the Trimorphic Protennoia there is a ritual with the help of which human beings are granted a gradual salvation or initiation and ascent into the realm of light. The entry into the sphere of eternal blessedness is preceded by various bestowals of heavenly gifts by each of three mythological figures. Here too there are five stages, comparable to the five baptisms in Zostrianos and the five seals in the Apocryphon of John (NHC II 1; 30,22ff.). The one who gives this promise on the ascent is the Gnostic revealer, a female figure.

(NHC XIII 1; 45,12ff.) And I am inviting you into the exalted and perfect light. Now when you enter into this, you will receive glory from those [who] give glory.
And those who give thrones will give you thrones.
You will accept robes from those who give robes.
And the baptists will baptize you.
And you will become exceedingly glorious, in the manner you were at the beginning, when you were *light*.

(NHC XIII 1; 48,11ff.) (...) And I put upon him a shining light, which is the knowledge of the thought of the fatherhood.

And I delivered him to those who give robes: Jammon, Elasso, Amenai. And they [clothed] him with a robe from the robes of the light.

And I delivered him to the baptists. And they baptized him: Micheus, Michar, Mnesinous. And they immersed him in the spring of the [water] of life.

And I delivered him to those who [give] thrones: Bariel, Nouthan, Sabenai. And they [gave] him a throne from the throne of glory.

And I delivered him to those who give glory: Ariom, Elien, Phariel. And they gave him glory in the glory of the fatherhood.

And those who snatch away snatched (him) away: Kamaliel, [...] anen, Samblo, the servants of *the* great holy enlighteners. And they transported him into the light-[place] of his fatherhood. And [he received] the five seals from [the Light] of the Mother, the Protennoia. And they [let] him partake of the [mystery] of knowledge, and [he became a light] in the light.

On baptism and salvation from the Tripartite Tractate

In the Tripartite Tractate there are many sections with a hymnic structure, which describe the Unknown Father (p.124), Christ (p.71), the thought of the Logos, knowledge, but also salvation and baptism and give them ever new names (cf. also 59,29ff.; 87,6ff.; 100,28ff.). Central motifs in the description of salvation and the processes connected with it like the return of the thought of the Logos and baptism are the notion of repose, of stability, of union, of light and of joy.

(NHC I 5; 71,23ff.) He (viz. the Father) has extended to them:
a faith and a prayer to the one whom they do not see,
and a firm hope in the one whom they do not understand,
and a fruitful love which looks into that which it does not see,
and an acceptable understanding of the eternal mind,
and a bliss which is riches and freedom,
and a wisdom of that which the glory of the Father wills for his thought.

(NHC I 5; 92,22ff.) The thought of the Logos, which has returned to his stability and ruled over those who came into being because of him, was called 'Aeon' and 'Place of all those whom he had brought forth in accordance with the determination'.

And it is similarly called 'synagogue of salvation', for it has healed itself from the dispersion which is manifold thought – and it returned to a single thought.

It is similarly called 'storehouse', because of the rest which it had received, which is given to it alone.

And it is similarly called 'bride', because of the joy of the one who gave himself in the hope of fruit from the union and who appeared to him.

It is similarly called 'kingdom' because of the stability which it has been given, in which it rejoices at its seizure of those who opposed it.

And it is called 'joy of the Lord' because of the jubilation in [which it] was clothed. With it is the light, giving it the reward for the good things which are in it. And (with it) is the thought of freedom.

(NHC I 5; 124,3ff.) It (salvation) is not only a release from the domination of the left ones, nor was it only a [flight] from the sphere of power of those of the right, to each of which we thought that we were slaves and sons, from which no one flees without quickly becoming their possession again.

Rather, salvation is also an ascent [to] the levels which are in the Pleroma and [to] those which have named themselves with names and which have understood themselves in accordance with the power of each of the aeons.

And (it is) an entering into that which is silent, where there is no need of voice or knowledge or understanding or illumination, but (where) all things are light, where they do not need to be illuminated.

(NHC I 5; 127,25ff.) As for the baptism which exists in the real sense, into which the allnesses will descend and in which they will remain – there is no other baptism than this alone, which is the salvation into God, the Father, the Son and the Holy Spirit, when confession is made through faith in those names, which are a single name of the gospel, when they (viz. the baptized) have come to believe in what has been said to them, namely that they exist. For from this they have their salvation, those who have come to believe that they exist. This now is the comprehending in invisibility of the Father and the Son and the Holy Spirit in a faith which is without doubt (...).

The baptism which we mentioned previously is called 'robe of those who do not strip themselves of it', for those who will put it on and those who have received salvation wear it.

It is also called 'the strength of the truth which has no fall'. In an unwavering and immovable way it grasps all those who have received the [restoration] while they grasp it.

(Baptism) is called 'silence' because of the quiet and the unshakeability.

It is also called 'bridal chamber' because of the agreement and the indivisible state of those who know they have known him.

It is also called 'the light which does not set and is without flame', since it does not give light, but those who have worn it have become light. They are the ones whom he wore.

(Baptism) is also called 'the eternal life', which is immortality; and it is called 'that which is, perfect, simple', in the real sense, what is pleasing, inseparably and irremovably and faultlessly and unshakeably, for the one who exists for those who have received an initiation. (...)

Survey of Gnostic sacraments

The church father and heresiologist Irenaeus gives a survey of Gnostic sacraments in the first book of his *Against the Heresies* (Irenaeus, *Haer.* I 21, 2ff.). Although the description of the sacraments does not come from an original Gnostic source, but is given by a heresiarch, in reality it comes very close to Gnostic spirituality. Irenaeus reports on Gnostic baptism, the bridal chamber, anointing and the sacrament of dying, including the tensions which existed among the Gnostics over the sacraments (see nn.69–71). The formulae recited by the Gnostics when performing the sacraments which Irenaeus hands down are particularly valuable. Here one could still be seeing an original Gnostic liturgy.

(21,2) They say that (viz. salvation) is necessary for those who have received perfect knowledge (gnosis), so that they will be reborn into the Most High Power. For otherwise it is impossible to reach the Pleroma, since in their view it is (viz. salvation) which leads down into the depths of Bythus. The baptism (instituted by the) Jesus who became visible is said to have been for the forgiveness of sins, but the salvation by that Christ who descended into him was for perfection. They assert that baptism is psychical, but salvation is pneumatic. And John is said to have proclaimed baptism with a view to repentance, whereas the salvation by Christ was brought to perfection. That is precisely what he means when he says, 'And I have another baptism to be baptized with, and I long very much for it.'[202] Moreover, they say that when the mother of the sons of Zebedee asked that they might sit, on the right hand and on the left hand with him in the kingdom, the Lord introduced this salvation to them by saying, 'Can you be baptized with the baptism which I shall be baptized with?'[203] And of Paul they assert that he expressly and often proclaimed salvation in Christ Jesus.[204] And that is what has been handed down by them quite differently and in discordant forms.

(21,3) Some of them prepare a bridal chamber and perform a secret festival with particular formulae for those who are being initiated; and they call it a pneumatic marriage which they are arranging, after the likeness to the syzygies of the world above. Others lead (the candidates) to the water, baptize them, and say: *'In the name of the Unknown Father of all things; in Truth, the Mother of all things; in Him who descended on Jesus for union and salvation and communion with the powers.'* Others utter Hebrew words, in order to make a greater impression on the initiates, as follows (Hebrew words follow). The translation is: *'I invoke that which is above every power of the Father (viz., the demiurge); it is called Light and good Spirit and Life, because you have ruled in the body.'* Others speak thus for the salvation: *'The name which is hidden from every deity and rule and truth, with which Jesus of Nazareth was clothed in the light zones of the Christ, who lives by the Holy Spirit for the heavenly salvation – this name of restoration (is)':* (Hebrew words follow). The translation is: *'I do not divide the spirit, the heart and the supercelestial, merciful power; I will rejoice in your name, (you) Saviour of truth.'* Such are the words of those who perform the initiation. The one who is being initiated replies, *'I have been made strong and I am saved, and I save my soul from this aeon and from all that belongs to it, in the name of Iao, who has saved his soul to salvation in the living Christ.'* Then all the bystanders say, *'Peace be to all on whom this name has descended.'* And then they anoint the initiated person with oil of balsam; for they think that this oil expresses that sweet fragrance which is above the All.

(21,4) However, some of them say that it is superfluous to bring persons to the water. They mix olive oil and water together with certain formulae similar to those already mentioned and pour this mixture on the heads of those to be initiated. In their view this is the salvation. But they similarly practise anointing with oil of balsam. Others reject all this and maintain that the mystery of the unutterable and invisible power may not be performed by visible and transitory things, nor that of inconceivable and incorporeal (forces) by visible and corporeal (things). The perfect salvation is the knowledge of the unutterable greatness. Whereas defect and suffering arose from ignorance, the whole state which caused the ignorance is dissolved by knowledge. Therefore gnosis is the salvation of the inner person. It is neither corporeal, for the body is indeed corruptible; nor is it psychical, since the soul also arose from a defect and is merely the abode of the spirit. The salvation must therefore be pneumatic. For through gnosis the inner, pneumatic self is saved. And with the knowledge of the All they are content. And that is said to be true salvation.

(21,5) There are yet others who redeem persons on the verge of death, by pouring olive oil and water on their heads, or also the unguent already mentioned, together with water and using the magical sayings mentioned above, so that they cannot be seized by the archons and the powers and become invisible. Thus their inner self ascends through the invisible spheres, while their body is left behind in the creaturely world and the soul is handed over to the demiurge. They also give them instructions for the situation after death. When they meet the powers they are to say: '*I am a son from the Father, the Father who already was before, and a son in the one who already was before. I have come to see all that is mine and what is alien – however, not completely alien, but it belongs to the Achamoth (the Sophia below), who is a woman and has made it for herself, but derives her gender from the one who already was before – and to return to what is mine, from where I went forth.*' They claim that when he says that, he escapes, and avoids the powers. He then comes to the companions of the demiurge, and he must say to them: '*I am a vessel more precious than the woman who created you. Though your mother may not know her own descent, I at any rate know*

*myself and know whence I am. And I call upon the incorrupt-
ible Sophia, who is in the Father, but is mother of your mother,
who has no father, nor any male pair. As woman born of
woman she has created you, without knowing her mother, and
in the belief that she was alone. But I call upon her mother.'*
When the companions of the demiurge hear these words, they
are greatly confused and make accusations against their origin
and their mother's descent. But they (viz., the dead Gnostics) go
into their own place, casting off their fetters, that is, the soul.

This is what we could discover about their salvation. But since
they differ among themselves both in doctrine and tradition,
and since those who join them are intent daily on inventing and
producing new things which no one has ever thought of, it is a
difficult matter to describe all their opinions.

Notes

1. Thus circumstantial clauses and participles are often translated as main clauses (see n.61). Moreover since a literal translation of the Coptic articles into English is not advisable for stylistic reasons, this has been dispensed with in favour of an appropriate turn of phrase.

2. For the rise of the catholic church in the second century see generally Gerd Lüdemann, *Heretics. The Other Side of Early Christianity*, 1996. The most important secondary literature is discussed here.

3. In Gnosticism, Pleroma means the totality of the aeons, i.e. the powers of the world beyond.

4. The *Excerpts from Theodotus* have been handed down in the Alexandrian theologian Clement of Alexandria (140/150 – 211/215). The *Excerpts* are regarded as a collection of sayings which come from a variety of Valentinian Gnostics including Theodotus. Such catalogues of questions as *ExTheod* 78, 2 are frequently attested in Gnostic texts (cf. Book of Thomas [NHC II 7; 138,8ff.], *Testimonium Veritatis* [NHC IX 3; 41,22ff.]) and in Gnostic revelation texts often introduce the appearance of the revealer (cf., e.g., The Hypostasis of the Archons [NHC II 4; 93,33ff.]; the Apocryphon of John [NHC II 1; 1,20ff.]).

5. Forerunners of the Mandaean scriptures are first attested in the early third century. It is very difficult to date the Mandaean texts precisely or to determine which doctrines or cultic formulae go back to old traditions. The dating of some sections of the Mandaean literature into the second or third century or some Mandaean traditions into the first (!) century CE is very bold and in the last resort cannot be verified. The pre-Christian dating of Mandaean traditions which is occasionally put forward is utterly wrong and purely speculative.

6. Mani gives an account of his life in the so-called Cologne Mani Codex; measuring only 3.5 by 4.5 cm, this codex is the smallest book from antiquity known to us. It dates from the fifth century and was probably produced in Egypt. In it Mani describes how he grew up in a Jewish Christian baptist sect going back to Elkesai. We also learn something about the revelations which were communicated to Mani by his heavenly twin brother. Lastly, the little work gives information about Mani's first missionary journeys.

If the Cologne Mani Codex is right in describing Mani's origin in the Jewish-Christian community of the Elkesaites, the Christian background to Manichaeism would be certain. However, historical scepticism about the historicity of the remarks in the Cologne Mani Codex is probably in place: although Mani relates his life in the first person singular, this book cannot really be attributed to him; the real author of the 'Confessions of Mani' remains unknown. For the literature on the Cologne Mani Codex see R. Cameron and A. J. Dewey, *The Cologne Mani Codex (P.Codex, inv.Nr. 4780), 'Concerning the Origin of His Body',* 1979.

7. Manichaeism lasted for almost 1000 years. This is not least because of its development of a church structure which most of the Gnostic associations lacked.

8. To fight the darkness (matter), the primal human being descends into the darkness. However, he is conquered by the prince of darkness and himself needs to be redeemed by the 'living spirit'. This notion of the 'saved Saviour' can be found in particular in the Psalms of Thomas. For literature on the Psalms of Thomas see P. Nagel, *Die Thomaspsalmen des koptisch-manichäischen Psalmbuches,* 1980. After being saved the primal human being works on the liberation of the sparks of light imprisoned in matter, which belong to him. These sparks of light correspond to the human soul.

9. Cf. e.g. the Kephalaia, penitential formulae, etc. However, our knowledge of the Manichaeans is not limited to their original sources; there is also information in the writings of their opponents – in an analogous way to the accounts of the Christian Gnostics in the heresiarchs and church fathers. Here the most important and influential accounts are those of the ex-Manichaean Augustine (354–430) in his *Confessions.*

Note generally the rich collection by J. Klimkeit, *Gnosis on the Silk Road. Gnostic Texts from Central Asia,* with an introduction which documents the present state of research on Mani and Manichaeism (1–26) and a bibliography (377–95); cf. also the monograph by S. N. C. Lieu, *Manichaeism in the Later Roman Empire and Medieval China,* WUNT 63, 1992; A. Böhlig, 'Manichäismus', *TRE* 22, 1991, 25–45. At present the literature on Manichaeism is overwhelming; as an example see only the works by P. Mirecki and J. BeDuhn (eds), *Emerging from Darkness. Studies in Recovery of Manichaean Sources,* NHMS 43, 1997; and S. N. C. Lieu, *Manichaeism in Central Asia and China,* NHMS 45, 1998.

10. As an example of more recent research on the Hermetica see G. Löhr, *Verherrlichung Gottes durch Philosophie. Der hermetische Traktat II im Rahmen der antiken Philosophie- und Religionsgeschichte,* WUNT 97, 1997, and R. v. d. Broek and W. J. Hanegraaf (eds.), *Gnosis and Hermeticism from Antiquity to Modern Times,* 1998. The real nature of the Hermetica is disputed. Sometimes the Hermetica have been regarded

as a religion, sometimes as a philosophical tendency. There are further questions: do the Hermetica originate in Egyptian, Jewish or Iranian religion, or are they completely in the tradition of Platonic philosophy? Did the Hermetists have a cult and rites, or are their writings 'desk' works, which do not reflect any real religious life? Were the Hermetists organized into cult communities or schools? Are the Hermetica to be seen as Gnosticism? Is there a 'higher' Hermetica (didactic philosophical treatises) and a 'lower' Hermetica (magical inscriptions, etc.)? What is important about the Nag Hammadi discovery for research into the Hermetica is that there are numerous references to the actual spirituality of the Hermetists: in the Hermetic writings in Codex VI, some of which were previously unknown (e.g. the Discourse on the Eighth and the Ninth [VI 6]), there are some references to the Hermetic practice of prayer and the Hermetic cult.

11. For a selection of literature see: B. Pearson, 'Gnosticism as Platonism', in id., *Gnosticism, Judaism and Egyptian Christianity*, 1990, 148–64; K. L. King, *A Revelation of the Unknowable God with Text, Translation, and Notes to NHC XI,3 Allogenes*, 1995; J. M. Robinson, 'The Three Steles of Seth and the Gnostics of Plotinus', in G. Widengren, *Proceedings of the International Colloquium on Gnosticism, Stockholm, August 20–25 1973*, 1977, 132–42; H.-M. Schenke, 'The Phenomenon and Significance of Gnostic Sethianism', in B. Layton (ed.), *The Rediscovery of Gnosticism. Vol.II: Sethian Gnosticism*, Studies in the History of Religions 41, 1981, 588–616; M. Tardieu, *Recherches sur la Formation de l'Apocalypse de Zostrien et les Sources de Marius Victorinus*, Res Orientales 9, 1996; J. D. Turner, 'The Gnostic Threefold Path to Enlightenment: The Ascent of Mind and the Descent of Wisdom', *NovT* 22, 1980, 324–51; also R. T. Wallis and J. Bergman (eds), *Neoplatonism and Gnosticism*, International Society for Neoplatonic Studies 6, 1992.

12. Exceptions are the works Melchizedek (NHC IX 1), Trimorphic Protennoia (NHC XIII 1) and the Untitled Text in the Bruce Codex. These texts have close similarities to Sethian Gnosticism, but have undergone a Christian revision.

13. Porphyry, *Vita Plotini* 16ff.: 'At that time there were many Christians and some others, and they (viz. the others) were sectarians who had departed from philosophy, pupils of Adelphius and Aquilinus. They were in possession of many writings of Alexander the Libyan, Philocomes, Demostratus and Lydos, and they quote from the revelations of Zoroaster, Zostrianos, Nikotheos, Allogenes and Messos, and others of this kind. They have led many astray, although they themselves are the ones who have gone astray(...).' For the basis of the translation see the edition by R. Harder, *Plotins Schriften, Band Vc: Anhang. Porphyrius. Über Plotins Leben und über die Ordnung seiner Schriften*, 1958.

14. Thus the writings Zostrianos (NHC VIII 1), Marsanes (NHC X 1)

and Allogenes (NHC XI 3) represent accounts of the ascent of the recipients of revelation; The Three Steles of Seth (NHC VII 5) make the ascent in spiritual form; cf. also the accounts of ascent in the Trimorphic Protennoia (NHC XIII 1), p.141.

15. For the persecution of the Gnostics by church Christians cf. e.g. the Apocalypse of Peter (NHC VII 3) or the Testimonium Veritatis (NHC IX 3).

16. Cf. also the eucharist in the Pistis Sophia which takes this further (cf. pp.109ff.).

17. Cf. also the strong polemic against water baptism in Gnostic writings like the Paraphrase of Shem (NHC VII 1; 36, 25ff.) or the Testimonium Veritatis (NHC IX 3; 69, 7ff.).

18. As an example, see the Apocryphon of John (NHC II 1; III 1; IV 1). Thus sections of the Gnostic system as developed in the Apocryphon of John resemble Irenaeus's account of particular Gnostic groups (Irenaeus, *Haer.* I 29). For the dating of the individual Nag Hammadi writings see the relevant passages in Gerd Lüdemann and Martina Janssen, *Bibel der Häretiker. Die gnostischen Schriften aus Nag Hammadi*, 1997. The literature on the Nag Hammadi writings is almost impossible to survey. The composite volume edited by J. D. Turner and A. McGuire, *The Nag Hammadi Library after Fifty Years. Proceedings of the 1995 Society of Biblical Literature Commemoration*, NHMS 44, 1997, documents a relatively recent state of research with an extensive bibliography. For the standard literature on the individual Nag Hammadi writings cited here cf. the bibliography by D. M. Scholer, *Nag Hammadi Bibliography 1948–1969*, NHS 1, 1971, and id., *Nag Hammadi Bibliography 1970–1994*, NHMS 32, 1997.

19. The Gnostic character of the Odes of Solomon is not undisputed by scholars. Even if the Syrian Christians who stand behind the Odes of Solomon cannot perhaps be called Gnostics in the full sense, their religion does display Gnostic features.

20. Thus for example there is an apocryphal 'Acts of the Apostles' among the Nag Hammadi writings used by the Gnostics with the title The Acts of Peter and the Twelve Apostles (NHC VI 1). An apocryphal narrative about Peter has also been preserved in the Berlin Codex, which contains predominantly Gnostic writings.

21. Mention should also be made of Bardesanes of Edessa (died 222) as a source for Gnostic piety. He communicated his gnosis-like teaching to his son Harmonios in 150 hymns; however, only part of these have been preserved in Ephraem the Syrian (306–373), and he does not usually reproduce his sources faithfully. Among other works, the Hymn of the Pearl from the Acts of Thomas (107ff.) and further hymns from apostolic Acts have been attributed to Bardesanes, but this can only be a conjecture.

For Bardesanes see e.g. H. J. W. Drijvers, *Bardaisan of Edessa*, Studia Semitica Neerlandia 6, 1966, esp. 143–52.

22. In Gnosticism women had essentially more rights than they did in the catholic church of the second century. As the character of the Gnostic movement and also Montanism is largely charismatic and prophetic, at that time it was impossible to overlook 'women with charismatic gifts'. A further reason for the major role played by women in Gnosticism can be the significance of the feminine element in Gnostic mythology and sacramental praxis: spiritualized feminine deities live on in the Gnostic myths, and the notion of the bride is a central theme in Gnostic sacramental practice (bridal chamber). Another possible reason for the large number of women in Gnosticism was the social situation. Women also worked as teachers in Gnosticism (e.g. Philumene as the teacher of Apelles, Tertullian, *Anim.*36, 2; Eusebius, *Church History* V 13, 2), in the sacral sphere (e.g. Marcus's women: Irenaeus, *Haer.* I, 13, 3ff.), they function as the founders of sects (cf. e.g. Marcellina, Irenaeus, *Haer.* I 25, 6ff.), and they were accorded quasi-divine worship (e.g. Noria among the Nicolaitans, Epiphanius, *Haer.* 29, 1). Women attached themselves to Gnostic teachers (cf. e.g. Irenaeus, *Haer.* I 13, 3ff.) and lived with them. Furthermore, female companions of Jesus appeared as recipients of revelations conveying secret teachings of Jesus. Thus for example Mariamne is cited as the recipient of the revelations of James the brother of the Lord (e.g. First Apocalypse of James, NHC V 3; 40,23ff.). Salome was also the recipient of revelations from Jesus (cf. e.g. Gospel of Thomas and Pistis Sophia). However, Mary Magdalene is given the pre-eminent role: many writings bear her name (cf. e.g. the 'Great Questions of Mary', Epiphanius, *Haer.*26, 8f.), and she is also strongly represented in the other Gnostic writings (e.g. Gospel of Thomas 114; Pistis Sophia; Gospel of Mary, etc.). For the appearance of women in Gnosticism in this book see also the Ode on Norea (pp.118ff.) and the text about Helen (pp.129f.).

23. Thus we have not cited for example the well-known Hymn of the Pearl from the Acts of Thomas. Nor have hymns which have been preserved in fragments, as handed down in Melchizedek (NHC IX 1) or Zostrianos (NHC VIII 1), been included.

24. The hymns and prayers have not been handed down in isolation as such; as a rule they must be extracted from other textual locations (here the exceptions are e.g. the Prayer of the Apostle Paul [NHC I 1] or the inscriptions on the bridal chamber, pp.100f. below). This is done on the basis of literary criteria (stylistic change, a break in content, quotation formulae, etc.), form-critical criteria (e.g. Gnostic catechisms as an independent genre; possible *Sitz im Leben*, etc.), or also multiple attestation of a textual sequence (cf. e.g. the independent attestation to parts of the

Christ hymn from the Acts of John [94–96] in Augustine *[Ep.237]*). Extracting poetic traditions from the context is made more difficult by the fact that while most of the Gnostic hymns and prayers have a hymnic structure, they do not follow the laws of Greek poetry (for example the inscriptions from the Via Latina, cf. pp.100f., are exceptions).

25. Cf. e.g. G. W. MacRae, 'Prayer and Knowledge of Self in Gnosticism', in id. (ed.), *Prayer in Late Antiquity and Early Christianity*, Tantur Yearbook 1978–79, 1981, 97–113. For collections of texts, etc., cf. M. Lattke, *Hymnus. Materialien zu einer Geschichte der antiken Hymnologie*, NTOA 19, 1991, 147ff., 243ff. For the hymn generally see K. Thraede, 'Hymnus', *RAC* 16, 1994, 915–46; T. Wolbergs, *Griechische religiöse Gedichte der ersten nachchristlichen Jahrhunderte 1: Psalmen und Hymnen der Gnosis und des frühen Christentums*, Beiträge zur Klassischen Philologie 40, 1971; J. Kroll, *Die christliche Hymnodie bis auf Klemens von Alexandrien*, Libelli 240, ²1968. Cf. also M. Hengel, 'Das Christuslied im frühesten Gottesdienst', in W. Baier et al. (ed.), *Weisheit Gottes – Weisheit der Welt (FS J. Ratzinger)*, I, St Ottilien 1987, 357–404, esp. 366ff. Cf. also the bibliographical details on individual Gnostic hymns, *ad loc.*

26. The God of the Old Testament is usually depicted in a very negative way in the Gnostic writings (cf. also n.154). He is ignorant about the heavenly world, which is above him, and is full of envy. This is clear from the protest exegesis of Gen. 1f. combined with Isa. 45.5. Here On the Origin of the World (NHC II 5; 103,2ff.) may serve as an example: 'Now when the heavens had consolidated themselves together with their powers and their whole administration, the archigenitor became arrogant (...) He was delighted and boasted continually, saying to them, "I need no one." And he said, "I am God, and there is none other beside me (Isa. 45.5)." And when he had said this, he sinned against all the immortals who gave answer (...) Then, when Pistis saw the godlessness of the great archon, she was filled with wrath. She was invisible. She said, "You are wrong, Samael – which means 'the blind God'. There exists an immortal man of light (...) He will trample you – just as potter's clay is trampled ..."'

27. For Sethian Gnosticism see pp.13f., 89ff. and nn.11–14.

28. A section from this hymn appears almost word for word in the writing Allogenes (NHC XI 3); cf. Apocryphon of John (NHC II 1) 3, 20–33 with Allogenes (NHC XI 3) 62,27–63,25. Probably this passage was an originally independent piece of tradition.

29. Literally: plural 'gods'.

30. The first part of this hymn displays great similarity in content and form to the hymn to God attributed to Gregory of Nazianzus (cf. W.Christ and M. Paranikas [ed.], *Anthologia Graeca Carminum Christianorum* 1871 [reissued 1963], 24). It is conceivable that the two texts used a com-

mon basis or basic form. There are also similar praises of the Unknown Father, for example in Kerygma Petri 2a (Clement of Alexandria, *Stromateis* VI 5,39).

31. The use of the Trishagion (Isa.6.3) occurs often in religious literature; cf. only the prayer from Poimandres (CH I), on p.34 and the prayer from Melchizedek (NHC IX 1) in n.72; for church hymnography see n.80.

32. For further Hermetic hymns to the Father see *Corpus Hermeticum* XIII, 8–9.

33. The Eighth and the Ninth refer to notions of spheres in late antiquity. The Eighth is traditionally the beginning of the divine sphere and the place where the soul wanders after death to find rest. The Ninth can be the sphere of the deity itself or the space between the Eighth and the deity itself.

34. Like all the revelation dialogues among the Nag Hammadi writings, the Discourse on the Eighth and Ninth performs the function of communicating knowledge or introduction (Eisagoge) and initiation into knowledge which is important for salvation.

35. Cf. Mark 4.14.

36. An instrument for striking, e.g. by the zither player.

37. For CH XIII generally see K. W. Tröger, *Mysterienglaube und Gnosis in Corpus Hermeticum XIII*, TU 110, 1971, and W. C. Grese, *Corpus Hermeticum XIII and Early Christian Literature*, 1979; for the hymns in particular see G. Zuntz, 'On the Hymns in Corpus Hermeticum 13', *Hermes* 83, 1955, 58–92 (= id., *Opuscula Selecta. Classica. Hellenistica. Christiana*, 1972, 150–77). Cf. also D. J. M. Whitehouse, *The Hymns of Corpus Hermeticum: Forms with a Diverse Functional History*, Diss. Cambridge, Mass. 1985.

38. Here the reference does not seem to be to a particular Gospel but to Jesus Christ himself; for this formulation see also Authentikos Logos (NHC VI 3; 35, 5f.).

39. Cf. e.g. A. Kehl, 'Beiträge zum Verständnis einiger gnostischer und frühchristlicher Psalmen und Hymnen', *JAC* 15, 1973, 92–119; J. Holzhausen, 'Ein gnostischer Psalm? Zu Valentins Psalm in Hippol. *Ref.* VI 37, 7', *JAC* 36, 1993, 67–80; B. Herzhoff, *Zwei gnostische Psalmen. Interpretation und Untersuchung von Hippolytus, Refutatio V 10, 2 and VI 37, 7*, Diss. Bonn 1973.

40. For the Gnostic Valentinus cf. above all C. Markschies, *Valentinus Gnosticus? Untersuchungen zur valentinianischen Gnosis mit einem Kommentar zu den Fragmenten Valentins*, WUNT 65, 1992. In his work, Markschies comes to the conclusion that Valentinus was not a Gnostic at all. Although one can hardly agree with his main thesis, the commentaries on the fragments of Valentinus offer a wealth of new insights.

41. This Gnostic trend is known above all from the reports of Hippolytus (*Ref.* V 6, 3–11, 1; X, 9, 1ff.) and belongs to the Gnostic systems which start from three (primal) principles. The name of this Gnosticism, which is strongly influenced by paganism, is derived from the Hebrew word for 'serpent' (*nahash*). The serpent becomes the symbolic beast for salvation, a view which is not limited to the Naassenes (cf. the Perates in Hippolytus *Ref.* V 12, 1–7). The serpent brings human beings knowledge (protest exegesis of Gen.3) and is sometimes identified with Christ.

42. Cf. generally J. Frickel, *Hellenistische Erlösung in christlicher Deutung. Die gnostische Naassenerschrift*, NHS 19, 1984.

43. The 'liturgical hymns' which celebrate the ascent of the soul in the hour of death until the burial display a definite structure. There are three collections of these liturgical hymns in the Ginza (e.g. LG II 38–47: 28 hymns). The hymns begin with a specific opening: 'I am a Mana (spirit) of the great life, I am a Mana of the great (and) mighty life, I am a Mana of the great life.' This opening is followed by questions of the soul like: 'Who has led me away from my homeland?' Then follows a section which is stamped by lamentation. After this lamentation the Uthra (= power, corresponding to the aeons) descends, comforts the soul and gives it the hope of imminent liberation.

44. On its ascent the soul must pass by various guardrooms. This ascent of the soul among the Mandaeans recalls the Gnostic sacrament of dying: here particular formulae and answers are impressed on the soul; it must know them in order to make its way past the archons.

45. The translations are based on M. Lidzbarski, *Ginza*, Quellen der Religionsgeschichte 13, 1925.

46. Cf. n.149.

47. Cf. n.150.

48. The invitation of the Uthras (= powers) to the soul is given in more detail below, with largely similar formulations in the Mandaean praise of the soul (ch.3).

49. The textual basis for the translation is the edition by M. Lidzbarski, *Mandäische Liturgien*, 1962.

50. The basis for the translation is C. R. C. Allberry, *A Manichaean Psalm-Book, Part II*, Manichaean Manuscripts in the Chester Beatty Collection, Vol. 2, 1938, 181f.

51. For these dialogues see e.g. P. Nagel, 'Der Dialog im manichäischen Psalter', in G. Wiessner and H.-J. Klimkeit (eds), *Studia Manichaica II, Internationaler Kongress zum Manichäismus*, Studies in Oriental Religions 23, 1992, 220–38: 230ff.

52. The textual basis for the translation is the same as in n.50, 182, 20ff.

53. This is already suggested by the distinctive introduction of PS IV (a christophany on the ocean); cf. also the name Aberamentho for Jesus, which is attested only in PS IV.

54. The psalms are explicitly designated as such, for example '... in that they expressed their repentance in the seventieth psalm' (ch.36). The rendering of the psalms in the Pistis Sophia is not complete, but has undergone a 'Gnostic revision'. Thus statements are deleted which are incompatible with Gnostic thought or do not correspond to the situation of the Pistis Sophia. For the Psalms in the Pistis Sophia see generally A. Kragerud, *Die Hymnen der Pistis Sophia*, 1967; M. Lattke, 'The Odes of Solomon in Pistis Sophia: An Example of Gnostic "Exegesis"', *East Asia Journal of Theology* 1:2, 1983, 58–69; G. Widengren, 'Die Hymnen der Pistis Sophia und die gnostische Schriftauslegung', *Liber Amicorum: Studies in honour of C. J. Bleeker*, Supplements to Numen XVIII, 1969, 269–81.

55. Authades = the self-sufficient, autonomous.

56. Literally: 'and because of the delusion of your light...'

57. Pair = matching of opposite sexes. The separation of the pair is the cause of the fall and corruption. Through union it achieves salvation (cf. also the sacrament of the bridal chamber).

58. For the reconstruction with a commentary cf. above all M. Marcovich, 'The Naassene Psalm in Hippolytus (*Haer.* 5.10.2)', in B. Layton (ed.), *The Rediscovery of Gnosticism, Vol.II: Sethian Gnosticism*, Studies in the History of Religions XLI, 1981, 770–8; cf. also Herzhoff, *Zwei gnostische Psalmen* (n.39 above).

59. In earlier research the journey into heaven or the ascent of the soul was regarded as a central dogma or even as the origin of Gnosticism, cf. e.g. W. Anz, *Zur Frage nach dem Ursprung des Gnostizismus. Ein religionsgeschichtlicher Versuch*, TU 15, 5, 1897; W. Bousset, *Die Himmelsreise der Seele*, 1901 (Libelli 71, 1960).

60. These contradictory statements recall Bronte (NHC VI 2, see pp.6off.) and Acts of John 94–96 (see 67ff.).

61. The following prayer is not explicitly designated as such in the Exegesis of the Soul. However, the parallel ordering of the seven successive circumstantial clauses could suggest liturgical usage. For the sake of readability the circumstantial clauses have been translated as main clauses, especially as in Coptic the circumstantial clauses are often regarded as independent sentences (cf. W. C. Till, *Koptische Grammatik*, ⁵1978, no.334). Similarly, in hymnic literature, participles or relative clauses are not used with a subordinate function, but are equivalent to predicates of nouns (cf. e.g. E. Norden, *Agnostos Theos*, 41956, 166ff.). There is a literal translation of the prayer in the Additional Material. Such penitential prayers of confessions of guilt occur frequently in the Nag

Hammadi writings at the end of a dissertation or homily (cf. e.g. the Apocalypse of Adam [NHC V 5] 83, 24ff.: 'But we have performed every deed in a misunderstanding of the powers. We have boasted about the transgression of [all] our deeds. We have [cried out] against God because of all his deeds [...]. But these are our spirits. For now we have come to know that our souls will die the death'). These passages are probably independent pieces of tradition and had their *Sitz im Leben* in the cult.

62. The wave probably refers to the situation of a shipwreck, which is also depicted in the Exegesis of the Soul, 136, 17ff.

63. In all probability Jeu here means the 'true God', the Father.

64. In Manichaeism, too, the primal human being must gather his scattered members of light or his soul (cf. e.g. Ceph.31: '(...) his members and gathers together his soul [...] the soul which has suffered through the enemy. They were gathered together and came, in that they were again established in the image of their Father'). For the notion of 'gathering' in Gnosticism see also the fragment of the Gospel of Eve handed down in Epiphanius, *Haer*. 26, 3, 1: 'I stood on a tall mountain and saw a tall man and another who was shorter and heard a voice like thunder and went closer to hear. Then he spoke to me and said, "I am you and you are me, and where you are there am I and (I) am sown in all; and whence you are, you gather me, and when you gather me you gather yourself"'; cf. also Irenaeus, *Haer*. I 30, 14, where the gathering is interpreted as an eschatological event; cf. also the Gospel of Philip in Epiphanius (see p.84) and the bridal hymn from the Acts of Thomas (see pp.101ff.).

65. Literally 'his' name (this also applies to the next paragraph); here translated by the second person singular for the sake of uniformity.

66. The beginning of the prayer has not been preserved; however, it is probable that aeons one to four were mentioned in the previous paragraphs.

67. Heavenly powers.

68. For bibliography see e.g. A. K. Hembold, 'Redeemer Hymns – Gnostic and Christian', in R. N. Longenecker and M. C. Tenney, *New Dimensions in New Testament Study*, 1974, 71–8; G. W. MacRae, 'The Ego Proclamation in Gnostic Sources', in E. Bammel (ed.), *The Trial of Jesus*, SBT II/13, 1970, 122–34.

69. E.g. F. C. Baur, *Die christliche Gnosis oder die christliche Religions-Philosophie in ihrer geschichtlichen Entwicklung*, Tübingen 1835 (reprinted Darmstadt 1967).

70. E.g. G. Koffmane, *Die Gnosis nach ihrer Tendenz und Organisation, Zwoelf Thesen*, Breslau 1881.

71. It is to be assumed that there is no uniform understanding of cultic actions in Gnosticism. Thus there will have been groups which spoke out clearly against cultic actions (cf. Irenaeus, *Haer*. I 21, 4), whereas on the

other hand, for example, the Marcosians and some Sethian trends were clearly stamped by sacramental experiences (for the literature cf. e.g. H.-G. Gaffron, *Studien zum koptischen Philippusevangelium unter besonderer Berücksichtigung der Sakramente*, Bonn theological dissertation 1969; J.-M. Sevrin, *Le dossier baptismal sethien: Etudes sur la sacramentaire gnostique*, BCNH. Section Etudes 2, 1986). However, an affinity to the mystery cults is at all events formal. The particular way to salvation differs: if in Gnosticism the concern is for human beings to recover their original divinity through knowledge and sacrament, in the mystery cults what takes place is a divinization of something which was not originally divine.

72. For further hymnic sections cf. e.g. Melchizedek NHC IX 1; 14,15–18,7. The prayer from Melchizedek, which is unfortunately in a bad state of preservation, is a baptismal prayer (14,15–16,16), to which is attached a probably independent praise of the great (16,16–18,7); this three times praises as holy the mythological entities of Sethian Gnosticism in verses with a similar form. Further prayers are to be found in the Dialogue of the Saviour (NHC III 5; 121,5–122,1) or in the Letter of Peter to Philip (NHC VIII 2; 133,121–134,9); here, however, they represent scriptural prayers and serve only the narrative context.

73. For the literature see R. v. d. Broek, 'Von der jüdischen Weisheit zum gnostischen Erlöser. Zum Schlusshymnus aus dem Apokryphon des Johannes', in id., *Studies in Gnosticism and Alexandrian Christianity*, NHMS 39, 1996, 87–116.

74. The underworld is the world in which human beings are. In view of the dualism between earthly and heavenly world which is present in Gnostic thought and feeling, this notion is not surprising and appears in many texts (e.g. the Trimorphic Protennoia [NHC XIII 1]) moreover the saving work of Christ is felt in Christian Gnostic texts to be a descent into the underworld (= world) (cf. The Teachings of Silvanus [NHC VII 4; 104, 2ff.;110, 14ff., cf. pp.74ff. and nn.86, 87]).

75. There are parallel formulations to Bronte (NHC VI 2) 13, 19ff. in On the Origin of the World (NHC II 5) 114, 7ff. (cf. The Hypostasis of the Archons, NHC II 4; 89, 14ff.). There it is the heavenly Eve who introduces herself to Adam with these words. In Bronte, however, the revealer is more a universal goddess who combines the features of Sophia and Eve; on Bronte 13, 19ff., cf. also Hippolytus, *Ref.* VI 17, 3: 'This is the one power divided above and below, begetting itself, multiplying itself, seeking itself, finding itself, its own mother, its own father, its own sister, its own wife, its own daughter, its own son, mother, father, one, the root of the All.'

76. Cf. such a feature also in the Mandaean Ginza (RG 207, 35ff.): 'I am the death, I am the life. I am the darkness, I am the light. I am the error,

I am the truth. I am the destruction, I am the building up. I am the blow, I am the healing' (said by Ewath of itself). However, it is a frequently observable phenomenon that religious talk is 'paradoxical talk'. For paradoxical talk as religious talk in modern times cf. e.g. Anon, *Das Testament des Vaters*, Potsdam 1922, 8f.: 'I comfort, I am uncomforted. I baptize, I am not baptized. I send, I am not sent (...) I beget, I am not begotten. I bless, I am not blessed. I bow, I am not bowed.' Cf. also Stefan George, *Der Stern des Bundes*, 1914, 21: 'I am the one and I am both, etc.'

77. Here the reading should probably be 'the going'.

78. That this Christ hymn is independent is also suggested by the fact that fragments of it have been handed down by Augustine in his Letter 237. As an example of the numerous works on the Christ hymn in the Acts of John see A. J. Dewey, 'The Hymn in the Acts of John. Dance as Hermeneutic', in D. R. MacDonald, *The Apocryphal Acts of Apostles*, Semeia 38, 1986, 67–80 (see also n.137).

79. Thus the composer Gustav Holst set it to music in 1917 (*Hymn of Christ*, op.37); for an example of a literary treatment of the Christ hymn see Marguérite Yourcenar, *L'ouvre au noir* (1968). The film producer Louis Buñuel also used a fragment of the Christ hymn which is contained in Augustine, *Ep*.237, in his film *La Voie Lactée* (1969).

80. Clement of Alexandria is the first to dispense with the composition of christological psalms. Some hymns to Christ by him have been handed down (e.g. *Paidagogos* 3, 101, 3; *Protreptikos* 11, 113, 3). For the literature cf. e.g. G. May, 'Der Christushymnus des Clemens von Alexandrien', *Liturgie und Dichtung* I, 1983, 257–73. As a further example of hymns to Christ composed by the church cf. K. Treu, 'Ein altkirchlicher Christushymnus (P.Berol. 16 389)', *NT* 19, 1977, 142–9. This hymn praises Christ as holy three times; the content is orientated on the creed. For further hymns cf. the literature in n.25 and also R. Messenger, *Christian Hymns of the First Three Centuries*, 1942; P. Plank, *Phos Hilaron. Christushymnus und Lichtdanksagung der frühen Christenheit*, Habilitationsschrift Würzburg 1985; G. Schille, *Früh-christliche Hymnen*, 1965.

81. There are many other hymns in the Nag Hammadi writings apart from those which are reproduced here. Cf. e.g. the hymnic section in the Second Apocalypse of James [NHC V 4] 58, 2ff. or the enumeration of the titles of Christ in the Teachings of Silvanus, which has a parallel structure, (NHC VII 4) 106, 21ff. Cf. also First Apocalypse of James (NHC V 3; 28,7).

82. Cf. the description of the crucifixion in the Apocalypse of Peter (NHC VII 3). In form this Nag Hammadi writing describes a revelation dialogue between Jesus and Peter; it has much in common with the Second Logos of the Great Seth (NHC VII 2: e.g. synousia between Gnostics and their Saviour, etc.). Thus in the Apocalypse of Peter (NHC VII 3) Peter is

granted a vision about the crucifixion (81.3ff.), which reads almost like a narrative accompaniment to the hymn in the Second Logos of the Great Seth (NHC VII 2):

(NHC VII 3; 81, 15ff.) 'The Saviour said to me, "The one whom you see above alongside the cross, joyful and laughing, is the living Jesus. But the one into whose hands and feet nails are driven is his bodily part, which is the substitute. They put to shame this, which came into being in his likeness. But look at him and me." And after I had looked, I said, "Lord, no one sees you. Let us flee from here." But he said to me, "'I have told you that they are blind. Depart from them. And see, they do not know what they are saying. For the son of their glory they have put to shame instead of my servant." And I saw how someone was about to approach us, who resembled him, and how the one who was by the cross laughed. And he was *full* of the Holy Spirit, and he is (was) the Saviour. And there was a great, indescribable light around them, and the multitude of indescribable and invisible angels praising them. And it was I who saw him when he was revealed as the one to whom praise was given.'

83. The notion that Simon of Cyrene (Mark 15 parr.) was crucified in place of Jesus is frequent in Gnosticism. Cf. Irenaeus's report on the docetic christology of the Gnostic Basilides (*Haer.* I 24,4): '(...) Therefore (they say that) he did not suffer, but compelled one Simon of Cyrene to bear the cross for him. He (viz. Simon) was transformed by him (viz. Jesus), so that he was taken for Jesus and was crucified out of ignorance and error. But Jesus assumed Simon's form, stood by and laughed at them. As he is an incorporeal power and the mind of the Father who did not come into being, he transformed himself as he will, and rose to the one who sent him. And he laughed at them (viz. the archons), as they could not hold him and he was invisible to all.'

84. Acts of John 101: 'You hear that I suffered, yet I did not suffer; that I did not suffer, yet I suffered; that I was pierced, and yet I was not struck; that I was hanged, and yet I was not hanged; that blood flowed from me, yet it did not flow; in short, that what those say of me I did not endure, but what they do not say, I suffered. But what it is I say to you in riddles, for I know that you will understand.'

85. In the apostle Paul's letter to the Philippians there is a hymn to Christ in two strophes which was originally independent (2.6–11); it describes the humiliation of the divine Christ (2, 6–8) and his exaltation (2, 9–11): '(1) Who, though he was in the form of God, did not count equality with God a thing to be held on to – like plunder – but emptied himself, taking the form of a servant. Being born in the likeness of men and being found in as it were human form he humbled himself, becoming obedient to death (...). (2) Therefore God has exalted him above all measure and bestowed on him by grace the name which is above all names,

that at the name of Jesus every knee should bow, of things in heaven and things on earth and things under the earth, and every tongue confess that Jesus Christ is Lord to the glory of God the Father.'

86. Cf. a Christ hymn from the Testimonium Veritatis (NHC IX 3; 32, 22–33,14): 'For the Son of [Man] clothed himself with their first-fruits. He went down into the underworld. And he performed many mighty acts. He raised the dead in it (viz. the underworld). And the world-rulers of the darkness burned (with anger) because of him, for they found no sin in him. Rather, he also destroyed their works among men. Likewise the lame, the blind, the paralysed, those possessed of demons – he gave them healing. And he walked upon the waters of the sea. Therefore he [destroyed] his (own) flesh [...] and he became [...] salvation [...] his death.'

87. This notion is also expressed in the first hymn from the Teachings of Silvanus (NHC VII 4; 103,34–104,14): 'Although he was God, he [was found] among human beings as a human being. He descended into the underworld. He released the children of death. They were in pain, as the scripture of God said, and he sealed its (the underworld's) heart. He broke its strong bows completely. And when all the powers saw him, they fled, so that he might bring you, who are to be pitied, from the depths and might die for you as a ransom for your sin. He saved you from the strong hand of the underworld.'

88. For the literature see M. L. Peel, 'The *"Decensus (sic!) ad Inferos"* in the "Teachings of Silvanus" (CG VII 4)', *Numen* 26, 1979, 23–49. In general: J. Kroll, *Gott und Hölle. Der Mythos vom Descensuskampfe*, 1932.

89. Cf. n.74.

90. Literally 'man', 'human being': the reference is to humankind generally.

91. Cf. the consubstantiality of the soul with the Saviour: 2, 35ff.; alienation in the world: 10,18ff.; imprisoned soul: 6,30ff.; contempt for the world: 1, 36ff.

92. In general the role of the church as the object of salvation is emphasized throughout the Interpretation of Knowledge: the church has its origin in heaven, but as a result of its fall is entangled in matter. Its salvation takes place through recollection of the origin (9,17ff.), which is communicated to it through Christ the teacher (13,33ff.). However, the function of Christ is not limited to teaching; his suffering also brings salvation, a notion which underlies the hymn in 10,27ff. (cf. also 12,23ff.).

93. From Inter 9, 16, Christ as teacher is the topic of the work. The author reports the teaching of Christ (cf. 9, 27: 'This is his teaching'; 10,18: 'For he said'). From 10, 21 the author admonishes his reader to accept the teaching of Christ, addressing her (the soul, the church) in the second person singular. From 10,27 on, the hymn follows, as an 'I am'

discourse. In contrast to the beginning, the end of the hymn cannot be ascertained, as the text breaks off from Inter 11, 1. It becomes legible again only after 11,15.

94. The reference to the side means the wound in Christ's side, which was inflicted on him at the crucifixion (cf. John 19.34). This is often identified (e.g. *ExTheod* 61, 3) with the wound inflicted on Adam when his rib was removed (Gen. 2.21ff.). The soul's (renewed) union with Christ comes about through the entry of the soul which is addressed in this hymn.

95. The burden is a reference to the body or 'the flesh of corruption' (Inter 10, 26f.).

96. Such an awakening call also occurs in the New Testament (Eph. 5.14): 'Awake you who sleep, and arise from the dead, and Christ will give you light.'

97. Or 'things that do not correspond to your being'; or 'unlike things'. The translation chosen here interprets the Coptic *anomoin* as a designation for the heresy of the Anhomoeans attested by Epiphanius (*Haer.* 76, 4, 7–9), since the definition of 'bad false teaching *(mntheresis)*' follows immediately afterwards in the text.

98. The word used, *mmalel*, contains echoes of the Syriac equivalent to the Logos.

99. The textual basis for the translation is the edition by W. Bauer, *Die Oden Salomos*, Kleine Texte für Vorlesungen und Übungen 64, 1933.

100. For the old man cf. e.g. Dan. 7.13: '(...) With the clouds of heaven there came one like a son of man. And he came to the Ancient of Days and was presented before him.'

101. Cf. Gal. 1.15.

102. Cf. Eph. 4.8; Ps. 68.19.

103. Really one would expect another answer to the old man's question 'Where do you come from?' (e.g. 'I come from the place where (...)'). Paul's answer fits the question 'Where are you going?' better.

104. The Gnostic catechism contained in the first Apocalypse of James has close parallels to Irenaeus' report on the Marcosian sacrament of dying (Irenaeus, *Haer.* I 21, 5, see Additional Material).

105. This Gospel of Philip is not identical with the Gospel of Philip from Nag Hammadi; see pp.139ff. and n.201.

106. For this witnessing formula see Paraphrase of Shem (NHC VII 1) 31, 4ff. There is a similar testimony by the revealer Derdekeas in 31,22ff., which is interpreted by him from 31,27 on and is explained to Shem.

107. The fourth archon Adonaios (cf. Origen, *Contra Celsum* VI 32) is absent from the text between Sabaoth (= fifth archon) and Astaphaios (= third archon).

108. The basis for the translation is P. Koetschau, *Origenes Werke*, Bd.2, *Buch V–VIII gegen Celsus. Die Schrift vom Gebet*, GCS 2, 1899.

109. Cf. W.-P. Funk, *Die zweite Apokalypse des Jakobus aus Nag-Hammadi-Codex* V, TU 119, 1976, 211–20.

110. This can already be inferred from the central significance of Seth. According to Gen. 4.25ff., Seth is the father of a new generation after the disastrous conflict beween Cain and Abel; in Sethian Gnosticism this generation is identified with the Gnostic generation. But the typical 'Sethian terminology' can also be found in the Three Steles of Seth (cf. e.g. 'living and unwavering generation', 'perfect individual', the triads 'Autogenes, Barbelo, Unbegotten Father' and 'Existence, Life, Mind', 'threefold male', etc.).

111. Thus the triad 'Existence, Life, Mind' was also widespread in late Greek philosophy. The title of the writing takes up the Jewish tradition of the 'two steles of Seth' (Josephus, *Ant.* 1, 67–71). The fact that this writing is about the '*Three* Steles of Seth' may be a result of Middle- or Neo-platonic influence, or is also simply to be attributed to an effort to do jus-tice to the Sethian triad 'Autogenes, Barbelo, Unbegotten Father'.

112. For a fundamental treatment see H. M. Schenke, 'The Pheno-menon and Significance of Gnostic Sethianism', in B. Layton (ed.), *The Rediscovery of Gnosticism, Vol. II : Sethian Gnosticism*, Studies in the History of Religions 41, 1981, 588–616. For further literature see n.11.

113. The Three Steles of Seth are attributed to Dositheos (118, 10ff.), but that should not lead us astray into relating Dositheos historically to Sethian Gnosticism as the (supposed) father of Samaritan Gnosticism (for Samaritan Gnosticism see S. J. Isser, *The Dositheans. A Samaritan Sect in Late Antiquity,* Studies in Judaism in Late Antiquity 17, 1976). Rather, the attribution of the revelations to Dositheos is to be attributed to the 'his-toricizing of the Saviour figure' which is often attested in the Nag Hammadi writings and is thus of a clearly later date.

114. 'I' can refer to Dositheos or Seth, but can also be understood as a 'liturgical I'.

115. Underlying both 'bless' and 'praise' is the Coptic word *smou*, which has both meanings. 'Praise' has been chosen for the suppliant, and 'bless' for God.

116. In the writing Allogenes (NHC XI 3), Allogenes receives revelations through visions and auditions which he hands on to his son Messos. Here in NHC XI 3; 54, 5ff., there is a similar praise to that in the Three Steles of Seth (the figure who utters the following hymn cannot be identified precisely; perhaps it is the revealer Joel): '(...)You are [...] Solmis [...]. According to the vitality [which is yours and] the first activity which derives from the deity. You are great, Armedon! You are perfect, Epiphaneu(s)!

And according to the activity of yours, the second power and the knowledge which comes from blessedness: Autoer, Beritheu(s), Erigenaor,

Orimeni(os), Aramen, Alphleges, Elelioupheu(s), Lalameu(s), Jetheu(s) Noetheu(s)! You are great! The one who knows [you] knows the Universal One. You are one, you are one; the one who is good, Aphredon! You are the aeon of aeons! You, who are at every time.'

Then she praised the Universal One, saying: 'Lalameu(s), Noetheu(s), Senaon, Asine[u(s), O]riphani(os), Mellephaneu(s), Elemaoni, Smoun, Optaon, He Who Is. You are He Who Is, the aeon of aeons, the unbegotten, you who are higher than the unbegotten ones, Jatomen(os), you alone, for? whom all the unborn ones were brought forth, the unnameable one.'

For similar invocations see also Zostrianos (NHC VIII 1) 49, 1ff.; 86, 13ff.; 88, 10ff.

117. The perfecting by stages is typical of (Sethian) Gnosticism; cf. Marsanes (NHC X 1; 2, 12ff.), Allogenes (NHC XI 3; 59, 4ff.), etc. In Marsanes (NHC X 1) the ascent by stages takes place in thirteen seals (= stages of knowledge). Cf. Marsanes (NHC X 1) 2, 16ff., where the ascent takes place from the first seal (= worldly/hylic) through the psychic, repentance, the mind, etc. up to the thirteenth seal, that 'above [the] Silent One who was not [known] and above the beginning of [the one who] was not distinguished' (5,19ff.). Cf. e.g. the spiritual ascent of Plotinus: 'Thus to precisely this demonic (= godlike) man often, when he raised himself up in his thoughts to the first God who is beyond (...), that God has appeared who has no shape and no form and is enthroned above the spirit and the whole spiritual world' (Porphyry, *Vita Plotini* 23, see n.13).

118. For the 'baptizers' and the following names cf. the Gospel of the Egyptians (NHC III 2) 64, 9ff.: '(Then) was revealed to them the great helper Jesseus Mazareus Jessedekeus, the living water, together with the great leaders James, the Great, and Theopemptos and Isavel and those who preside over the true fountain, Micheus and Michar and Mnesinous and the one who presides over the baptism of the living, and the purifiers, and Sesengenpharanges and those who preside over the gates of the water, Micheus and Michar, and those who stand on the mountain, Seldao and Elainos, and the receivers of the great generation, incorruptible, strong men *of* the great Seth.'

119. The meaning is probably that Zostrianos is inscribed in a 'book of glory' (cf. the Gospel of Truth [NHC I 3] 19, 28ff.: book of the living or in a 'light of glory' (cf. e.g. The Concept of Our Great Power [NHC VI 4] 36, 15ff.: great light).

120. There follows a lengthy section in which Zostrianos receives teachings in revelation dialogue and through visions. It is not until 53, 15ff. that the fifth baptism takes place.

121. The Gospel of the Egyptians from Nag Hammadi is a document of mythological Gnosticism: this writing is shaped by the hymn of praise

and the prayer of mythological entities along with letter and number mysticism. It shows close similarities to Sethian Gnosticism in the structure of the heavenly world, the identity of the heavenly entities and in cosmogony. This Nag Hammadi document has nothing in common with the Gospel of the Egyptians handed down by Clement of Alexandria in the *Stromateis* apart from its title. The latter work is a conversation between Jesus and his disciples after the resurrection with a marked Encratite stamp.

122. See also pp.94f. and n.118.

123. The Gnostic Neo-Platonic writing Marsanes (NHC X 1) and the Valentinian disciple Marcus (cf. pp.122, 105 and note) are two particularly prominent examples of a magical system of letters.

124. The last two lines also represent a sequence of vowels: *uaei eisaei eioei eiosei*. The translation offered in the text sees Greek words in this sequence of vowels.

125. Luke 10.19.

126. There is a similar structure of transforming false existence into true existence in Zostrianos (NHC VIII 1: 12, 10ff.): '(...)(and) from the antitype of exile up to the exile which really exists; (and) from the antitype of repentance up to the repentance which really exists; (and) [from the] antitype of the Autogenes [up to the Autogenes] which really exists (...)!' Cf. a similar formula which does not describe salvation but the consequences of the fall, from the Tripartite Tractate (NHC I 5) 80, 11ff.: 'The Logos was a cause of those [who] came into being, and he dwelt more and more, he was confused; and he was beside himself: instead of a perfection he saw a defect; instead of a mixture he saw a separation; instead of a stability he [saw] shakings; instead of [rest] (he saw) unrest.'

127. The literal translation of the name of the saviour 'Manda dHaije' is 'knowledge of life'.

128. *nsab*, literally 'he planted', occurs frequently with the meaning 'created'; it is the name of a spirit of life.

129. The eggs denote the mythical dwelling places of the souls.

130. The textual basis for the translation is M. Lidzbarski, *Mandäische Liturgien*, 1962.

131. For the text and commentary see P. Lampe, *Die stadtrömischen Christen in den ersten beiden Jahrhunderten. Untersuchungen zur Sozialgeschichte*, WUNT II 18, ²1989, 257ff.

132. This is probably an allusion to Valentinian celebrations of the eucharist; cf. also p.104.

133. For literature see e.g. H. Kruse, 'Das Brautlied der syrischen Thomasakten', *Orientalia Christiana Periodica* 50, 1984, 291–330; G. Gerleman, 'Bemerkungen zum Brautlied in den Thomasakten', *Annual of the Swedish Theological Institute 9*, FS H. Kosmala, 1974, 14–22.

134. 'Choose' or 'explain' are both possible translations for *mparesh* (literally 'distinguish, mark out').

135. In a transferred sense the word *niha* can also mean 'good pleasure'.

136. The textual basis for the translation is the edition by W. Bauer, *Die Oden Salomos* (see n.99).

137. For the liturgical material in the Acts of John cf. also R. H. Miller, 'Liturgical Materials in the Acts of John', *Studia Patristica* XIII, TU 116, 1975, 375–81.

138. Name for Jesus in the fourth book of the Pistis Sophia.

139. Cf. Luke 12.49.

140. Cf. John 4.10.

141. Cf. Matt.26.28.

142. Cf. John 19.34.

143. Cf. Matt.3.11; Luke 3.16.

144. Cf. Mark 12.25; Gal. 3.28.

145. For the questing religion of the Gnostics, at which the church Christians took offence, see e.g. K. Koschorke, 'Suchen und Finden in der Auseinandersetzung zwischen gnostischen und kirchlichen Christen', *WuD* NF 14, 1977, 51–65.

146. For the textual basis for the translation see nn.50 and 51, 197, 65ff.

147. The meaning is that the soul is concerned with a correct interpretation of the Gospels, in other words is engaged in Bible study.

148. The basis for the translation is the edition by M. Lattke, *Die Oden Salomos in ihrer Bedeutung für Neues Testament und Gnosis*, Band 1a, OBO 25/1a, 1980.

149. Mandaean 'Uthras' are light beings or angelic beings which correspond to the aeons.

150. Mandaean 'Skinas', literally 'dwelling places'. In the rabbinic Jewish sphere Skina denotes the presence of God in the temple or the world.

151. The textual basis for the translation is M. Lidzbarski, *Mandäische Liturgien*, 1962.

152. In Papyrus Mimaut col. XVIII, 591–611, the Hermetic prayer is part of a longer prayer in a magical text; in CH Asclepius 41b it represents the conclusion of the tractate. In Nag Hammadi Codex VI the prayer comes after the Discourse on the Eighth and Ninth and is occasionally regarded as its conclusion.

153. Norea is the subject of numerous Sethian writings; cf. e.g. The Hypostasis of the Archons (NHC II 4); cf. also On the Origin of the World (NHC II 5): 'the First Book of Norea (102, 10f.)', 'the first discourse of Norea' (102, 24f.).

154. However, the Gnostics also criticized the church Christians. They

accused them of sticking at the lowest level of truth and not seeking higher knowledge. This refers above all to the understanding of the Old Testament with its creator God, whom the Gnostics identified as the defective demiurge. In addition to the protest exegesis of the Old Testament which runs through all Gnostic writings (e.g. the positive interpretation of the fall), there is a document in the Second Logos of the Great Seth (NHC VII 2) which makes clear the Gnostic repudiation of the Old Testament: the hymn from the Second Logos of the Great Seth (62, 27–65,1) mocks the great figures of the Old Testament in strophes each of which is formulated in the same way. The stringing together and enumeration of the great figures of the Old Testament and figures from primal history (Adam, Abel, etc.), patriarchs (Abraham, etc.), prophets and kings occurs frequently (Sir. 44.1–15; 49.3–13; Wisdom 10; Heb. 11). Here, in contrast to the Gnostic hymn, the assessment is always positive. A further point of Gnostic criticism of the church Christians is their understanding of the crucifixion of Jesu, which they see as real, in contrast to the Gnostic docetism (see pp.72f.). The Gnostics also criticize the ministries of the church (cf. only the Apocalypse of Peter [NHC VII 3, 73, 11ff.; 76, 23ff.]: 'And others will arise who are not numbered among us, who call themselves "bishop" and also "deacon", as if they had received their authority from God. They submit to the judgment of the leaders. They are waterless pits', 79.22ff. For the whole problem see the standard investigation by K. Koschorke, *Die Polemik der Gnostiker gegen das kirchliche Christentum*, NHS 12, 1978.

155. The motifs of the polemic like eating children and knocking over the lampstand are first attested by Justin *(Apol.* I 26, 7). At this point Justin is taking up the accusations of educated pagans against the Christians. He disputes that such things take place among orthodox Christians, but does not rule out the possibility that these practices are current among the Gnostics. Thus at a very early stage the moral charges of sexual dissipation or the devouring of children is associated with the Gnostics.

156. An orator from Cirta in North Africa who according to Minucius Felix delivered a speech against the Christians.

157. The textual basis is B. Kytzler, *Minucius Felix, Octavius*, 1965.

158. This nickname was already given to the legendary Gnostic 'Simon Magus' (Acts 8.10). According to the polemical accounts of many church fathers, all the later heads of Gnostic schools derive from Simon Magus. For the Gnostic Marcus cf. generally the monograph by N. Förster, *Markus Magus*, Göttingen theological dissertation 1997 (to be published in WUNT).

159. Fallen angel.

160. Alongside Rome and Antioch, Alexandria was one of the three

world cities in late antiquity. Like Athens, this important trading city was regarded as a centre of education (the library of Alexandria). So it is not surprising that Alexandria was an important city for philosophers, theologians and philosophers of religion. Many religions and spiritual trends came together here: alongside the ongoing existence of Egyptian religion (the Isis-Osiris cult) among the indigenous population, Alexandria was a centre of Hellenistic Diaspora Judaism; Neoplatonism was founded in Alexandria in the second century by the former Christian Ammonius Saccas and developed there in the third century by Plotinus, Origen and Porphyry.

161. For Valentinus see n.40; for Basilides the monograph by W.A. Löhr, *Basilides und seine Schule. Zur Theologie- und Kirchengeschichte des zweiten Jahrhunderts*, WUNT 83, 1992.

162. (Flav.Vop. VII): 'There are the Egyptians, as you are well aware, inflated, wild, boastful, unjust and really dissolute men, curious about novelties even in their public songs, versifiers, producers of epigrams, mathematicians, soothsayers, doctors. Among them are Christians and Samaritans and those who at any time are discontented with the present, although they are free. But so that none of the Egyptians becomes angry with me, because he believes that what I write is only my own work, I present one of Hadrian's letters, taken from the books of one of his freemen, Phlegonis, which fully discloses the way of life of the Egyptians.' It is striking that the appetite for novelties is seen negatively, as in the church fathers' polemic against the Gnostics, in complete opposition to the Gnostic religious quest.

163. The basis for the translation is D. Magie, *The Scriptores Historiae Augustae* III, 1922, 398f. In this collection of Lives of Roman rulers (from Hadrian to Carinus), Flavius Vopiscus is one of six different 'biographers' in all. However, the Roman orator and historian Flavius Vopiscus, who dates from the fourth century after Christ, is not really the author of the Lives of the emperors, but only a pseudonym for an unknown author.

164. Thus there are great similarities to the teachings of Heracleon and those of Ptolemaeus, the *Excerpta ex Theodoto*, Irenaeus, *Haer.* I 1–8, and further Valentinian writings and notions. However, it is striking that the Tripartite Tractate does not seem to have the feminine partner (e.g. Sige, Charis) which is frequent in Valentinian Gnosticism. Because of the strong common features here with the Valentinian teacher Heracleon, he has been regarded as the author of the Tripartite Tractate. Of the Nag Hammadi writings, the Gospel of Truth (NHC I 3), the Gospel of Philip (NHC II 3), the Interpretation of Knowledge (NHC XI 1) and the Valentinian Exposition (NHC XI 2) are particularly close to the Tripartite Tractate.

165. Tripartite Tractate (NHC I 5) 76,2ff. : 'The intent, then, of the Logos, which is this, was good. When he had come forth, he gave glory to

the Father, even when something was added which lay beyond (his) possibility. He wanted to bring forth a perfect one from an agreement in which he had not been without having the command.'

166. A further approximation to the idea of God among the church Christians is the lack of a feminine parallel to God (cf. e.g. Sige [= Silence] or Charis [= Grace] in Valentinian Gnosticism). In this way the unity of God is emphasized. Such a lack of a feminine parallel in the Gnostic notion of God is not limited to the Tripartite Tractate; Irenaeus and Hippolytus also report about such Gnostics (Hippolytus, *Ref*.VI 29, 2–8; cf. Irenaeus, *Haer*. III 11, 5).

167. This title probably means 'Exegesis of the holy scriptures respecting the soul'.

168. Another possible translation is 'that they may acknowledge/know him'.

169. Jer. 3.1–4 LXX.

170. Hos. 2.4–9.

171. Ezek. 16.23–26.

172. Cf. Acts 15.20, 29; 21.25; I Thess. 4.3; I Cor. 6.18; II Cor. 7.1; Acts 15.13.

173. I Cor. 5.9–10.

174. Eph. 6.12.

175. Gen. 2.24b.

176. Gen. 3.16b; I Cor. 11.3; Eph. 5.23.

177. Ps. 44.11 LXX.

178. Gen. 12.1.

179. II Cor. 3.6; John 6.63.

180. Ps. 102.1–5 LXX.

181. John 6.44.

182. Matt. 5.4, 6.

183. Luke 14.26.

184. Mark 1.4; Acts 13.24.

185. I Clem. 8.3.

186. Isa. 30.15 LXX.

187. Isa. 30.19f. LXX.

188. Jer. 17.10.

189. Homer, *Odyssey* 1, 48–59.

190. Ibid., 4, 260–1.

191. Ibid., 4, 261–4.

192. Ps. 6.6–9 LXX.

193. A word of unknown origin which means 'ritual piece of bread'. Therefore the translation 'host' seems appropriate.

194. The reference is to God.

195. The word for mercy and (daily) prayer is synonymous here.

196. The text follows another version of the preceding texts.

197. The guardrooms are places between the earthly world and the beyond which serve to purify the soul and are under the supervision of demons.

198. The translation is based on M. Lidzbarski, *Ginza,* Quellen der Religionsgeschichte 13, 1925.

199. There is also a fragment of the Gospel of Truth in Codex XII.

200. However, a quotation from a Gospel of Philip (see above, p.84) is attested in Epiphanius, *Haer.* 26, 13, 2–3, which does not appear in the Coptic Gospel of Philip. But the ascent of the soul through the spheres of the archons after death presupposed in Epiphanius also occurs in the Coptic Gospel of Philip. Furthermore in Pistis Sophia 42 there is an indirect reference to Philip as the author of discourses of Jesus (together with Matthew and Thomas).

201. This becomes clear, for example, from sayings 32 and 55, where Mary is designated the pair consort of Jesus – as in Valentinianism. There could also be a reference in saying 39 to the Sophia Achamoth known from Valentinian texts.

202. Cf. Luke 12.50.

203. Cf. Mark 10.38.

204. Cf. Rom. 3.24; Eph. 1.7; Col. 1.14.

Sources

The textual basis for the translation of the Coptic Nag Hammadi texts, as
for the Pistis Sophia and the writings of the Bruce Codex, is the editions of
Nag Hammadi and Manichaean Studies (formerly *Nag Hammadi Studies*,
1971ff.). For the texts from the apostolic Acts (Acts of Thomas and Acts
of John), where no other indication is given reference was made to the edition by M. Bonnet, *Acta Apostolorum Apocrypha* II, 1+2, 1959. The edition by N. Brox, *Irenaeus von Lyon, Epideixeis. Adversus Haereses*, I,
FChr 8/1, 1993, served as the basis for the text of the church father
Irenaeus. Where they do not come from the Nag Hammadi codexes, the
edition by A. D. Nock and A. J. Festugière, *Corpus Hermeticum*, 1960ff.,
was used for the Hermetic writings. The basis for the translations of the
writings of the church father Epiphanius of Salamis was the edition by K.
Holl, *Epiphanius 1, Ancoratus und Panarion haer. 1–33*, GCS 25, 1915,
and *Epiphanius 2, Panarion haer. 34–64*, GCS 31, 1922. The textual edition by M. Marcovich, *Hippolytus, Refutatio omnium haeresium*, PTS 25,
1986 was used for the church father Hippolytus. The sources which
appear only once in this volume are indicated at the relevant place.

General literature on Gnosticism

W. Bauer, *Orthodoxy and Heresy in Earliest Christianity*, 1971

U. Bianchi (ed.), *Le Origini dello Gnosticismo, Colloqui di Messina 13–18 April 1966*, SHR 12, 1966

A. Böhlig, *Gnosis und Synkretismus. Gesammelte Aufsatze zur spätantiken Religionsgeschichte* I, II, WUNT 47, 1989

— and C. Markschies, *Gnosis und Manichäismus: Forschungen und Studien zu Texten von Valentin und Mani sowie zu den Bibliotheken von Nag Hammadi und Medinet Madi*, BZNW 72, 1994

W. Bousset, *Hauptprobleme der Gnosis*, FRLANT 10, 1907

R. v. d. Broek, *Studies in Gnosticism and Alexandrian Christianity*, NHMS 39, 1996

N. Brox, *Offenbarung, Gnosis und gnostischer Mythos bei Irenäus von Lyon. Zur Charakteristik der Systeme*, SPS 1, 1966

R. Bultmann, *Primitive Christianity in its Contemporary Setting*, [16]1972

C. Colpe, 'Heidnische, jüdische und christliche Überlieferung in den Schriften aus Nag Hammadi I–X', *JAC* 15, 1972 – JAC 25, 1982

E. de Faye, *Gnostiques et Gnosticisme: Étude critique des documents du gnosticisme chrétien aux IIe et IIIe siècles*, [2]1925

M. Franzmann, *Jesus in the Nag Hammadi Writings*, 1996

I. Gruenwald, *From Apocalypticism to Gnosticism: Studies in Apocalypticism, Merkava Mysticism and Gnosticism*, Beiträge zur Erforschung des Alten Testaments und antiken Judentums 14, 1988

C. W. Hedricki and R. Hodgson (eds.), *Nag Hammadi, Gnosticism and Early Christianity*, 1986

H. Jonas, *Gnosis und spätantiker Geist. Erster Teil: Die mythologische Gnosis*, FRLANT 35, [4]1988

—, *Gnosis und spätantiker Geist. Zweiter Teil: Von der Mythologie zur mystischen Philosophie*, erste und zweite Hälfte, ed. K. Rudolph, FRLANT 159, 1993

—, *The Gnostic Religion*, 1963

K. L. King, *Images of the Feminine in Gnosticism*, Studies in Antiquity and Christianity, 1988

Helmut Kœster, *Introduction to the New Testament. Vol. I: History,*

Culture, and Religion of the Hellenistic Age, ²1995; Vol. II: *History and Literature of Early Christianity,* 1987

Klaus Koschorke, *Die Polemik der Gnostiker gegen das kirchliche Christentum,* NHS 12, 1978

M. Krause (ed.), *Essays on the Nag Hammadi Texts in Honour of A. Böhlig,* NHS 3, 1972

— (ed.), *Gnosis and Gnosticism,* NHS 8, 1977

— (ed.), *Gnosis and Gnosticism,* NHS 17, 1981

B. Layton (ed.), *The Rediscovery of Gnosticism, Vol.1: The School of Valentinus,* 1980; Vol. II: *Sethian Gnosticism,* 1981 (= *Proceedings of the International Conference of Gnosticism at Yale, New Haven, Connecticut, March 28–31, 1978*).

—, *The Gnostic Scriptures. A New Translation with Annotations and Introductions,* 1987

S. R. C. Lilla, *Clement of Alexandria: A Study in Christian Platonism and Gnosticism,* Oxford Theological Monographs, 1971

A. H. B. Logan, *Gnostic Truth and Christian Heresy,* 1996

G. Lüdemann, *Heretics. The Other Side of Early Christianity,* 1996.

– and Martina Janssen, *Bibel der Häretiker. Die gnostischen Schriften aus Nag Hammadi,* 1997

M. Markovich, *Studies in Graeco-Roman Religions and Gnosticism,* Studies in Greek and Roman Religion 4, 1988

G. R. S. Mead, *A Faith Forgotten. A Contribution to the Study of the Origins of Christianity,* 1960

Robert J. Miller (ed.), *The Complete Gospels,* 1994

Elaine Pagels, *The Gnostic Gospels,* 1980

B. A. Pearson, *Gnosticism, Judaism, and Egyptian Christianity,* Studies in Antiquity and Christianity, 1990

P. Perkins, *The Gnostic Dialogue: The Early Church and the Crisis of Gnosticism,* 1980

—, *Gnosticism and the New Testament,* 1993

S. Petrement, *A Separate God: The Christian Origins of Gnosticism,* 1990

G. Quispel, *Gnosis als Weltreligion,* ²1972

K. Rudolph, *Gnosis. The Nature and History of Gnosticism,* 1983

—, *Gnosis und spätantike Religionsgeschichte. Gesammelte Aufsätze,* NHMS 42, 1996

D. M. Scholer, *Gnosticism in the Early Church,* Studies in Early Christianity 5, 1993

M. Scopello, *Les gnostiques,* 1991

G. G. Stroumsa, *Another Seed: Studies in Gnostic Mythology,* NHS 24, 1984

K. W. Tröger (ed.), *Gnosis und Neues Testament,* 1973